# SEA RAIDS
# AND RESCUES

# SEA RAIDS AND RESCUES

## The United States Coast Guard

*Madelyn Klein Anderson*

David McKay Company, Inc.
New York

**Photos courtesy of United States Coast Guard.**

Library of Congress Cataloging in Publication Data

Anderson, Madelyn Klein.
  Sea raids and rescues.

  Includes index.
  SUMMARY: Presents a history of the Coast Guard from
the late 1700's to the present. Includes stories of
their feats in dealing with pirating, illegal
fishing, and shipwrecks.
  1. United States. Coast Guard—History—Juvenile
literature.  [1. United States. Coast Guard—History]
I. Title.
VG53.A53     359.9'7'0973     78-20297
ISBN 0-679-20951-4

1 2 3 4 5 6 7 8 9 10
Manufactured in the United States of America

To my parents and Justin—
different kinds of lifesavers.

# ACKNOWLEDGMENTS

I am deeply indebted to Dr. Robert L. Scheina, United States Coast Guard Historian, for his unflagging patience and efforts in supplying source material and reading the manuscript for accuracy; to Elizabeth A. Segedi, former photo librarian at Coast Guard headquarters in Washington, D.C., for opening her files to me; to Lt. Kent E. Fisher for allowing me to use his *Spartan Lady* diary; to chief Paul C. Scotti for keeping me supplied with material, including the *Cigale* story, and pictures—not to speak of moral support; and to all the men and women of the Coast Guard, both civilian and military, whose courtesies have been numerous and wonderful.

# CONTENTS

# SEA RAIDS
# AND RESCUES

# *1*

# *SMUGGLERS AND PIRATES*

The rocky beaches of Oregon offer great fishing and duck hunting. Late in 1977, when a newcomer to a southern Oregon town fenced off his farm and deprived his fishing and hunting neighbors of the only access road to the beach for miles around, they did not take it kindly. They knew he was within his rights, but why should he want to inconvenience everyone? People began talking about the man's seclusiveness, and then about the strange sounds coming from the area.

Rumors reached the Customs Patrol Officer, who did a little investigating and felt that all was not as it should be. But his feeling was just a hunch. However, he asked the Coast Guard to make a helicopter survey of the farm. Aerial photos showed wide tire tracks. The Customs officers searched the beach and found the same tracks. They were of a size that could belong to a World War II "duck," an amphibious vehicle. A duck might mean a mother ship—and a possible smuggling operation.

These little shreds of suspicion led to surveillance by customs agents, state and local police, and the Coast Guard. An observation post was set up a few miles from the farm, and special night vision devices were used for observation. A week

*The* Cigale *under tow.*

of surveillance turned up nothing. The Coast Guard flew another helicopter survey. Still nothing. Nothing, that is, until the aerial photographs were developed and revealed what human eyes could not see: a tractor trailer hidden in the trees.

It certainly seemed that something was going on, but nobody could be certain it was smuggling. So, quietly, surveillance was widened.

A C-130 aircraft on a search and rescue mission for an overdue fishing boat was told to keep an eye out at the same time for any suspicious vessels. It found a survivor of the fishing boat adrift in a life raft, but no suspicious vessels.

Still the surveillance continued. Then, on December 29, there seemed to be some movement at the farm. And a ship, the *Cigale,* was moving in the area. It looked as if a rendezvous was about to take place. Personnel at the Coast Guard Air Station opened sealed orders containing a full briefing and the special radio frequencies to use for coordination so that no transmissions could be intercepted by the suspects. A helicopter was dispatched, showing no lights and making no radio transmissions. At the Coast Guard lifeboat station nearby, weapons were broken out. The 52-foot motor lifeboat *Intrepid* took off—supposedly on a rescue mission—so that radio contact could be maintained by a code using rescue terms.

And then there was a light on the horizon. The suspect vessel was spooked and gone, and everybody and everything went back to their stations.

But in the early morning hours of New Year's Eve, the alert was on again. More helicopters this time, plus a C-130 sent from San Francisco and the cutters *Modoc* and *Cape Carter*. The county SWAT team—specially-trained police officers—and sheriff's deputies joined Customs, Drug Enforcement Administration Station agents, and Coast Guard personnel to make up a massive ground-air-sea force.

Night vision devices and walkie talkies established the fact that there were at least *two* ducks, and it was decided to take them when they were ashore. The helicopters circled north of the area, waiting for a flare to tell them when to move in. Then, at 4:48 A.M., one red flare, and the first helicopter moved in, flashed its lights on, and lit the area with its searchlight. Now the second helicopter joined up.

On the ground, men scattered in a frenzy, with ground personnel in hot pursuit. Searchlights of the helicopters illumined the scene. One of the helicopters was fired on, and it answered with automatic rifles and shotguns.

At sea, the pursuit boats moved out from behind the rocks where they had hidden from *Cigale*'s radar. The *Cigale*'s crew began chucking bales of some kind of material overboard. Pursued by the *Intrepid,* the *Cigale* started moving peculiarly, as though she were without guidance at the helm. A boarding party from the *Intrepid* made a tricky leap onto

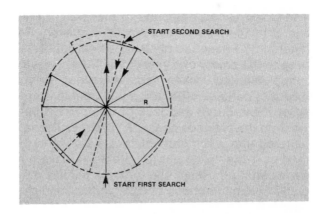

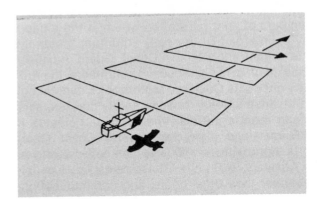

*This diagram shows how U.S. Coast Guard
surface units perform "trackline searches," while
aircraft run coordinated "creeping line" patterns.*

the moving *Cigale*. A quick search soon showed that the *Cigale* had been abandoned and scuttled; there was over five feet of water in her hold. Damage-control crews from the *Intrepid* and the *Modoc* worked furiously in shoulder-high water to mend pipes the smugglers had cut. Finally, the flooding was stopped and the vessel was pumped dry.

4

The *Cigale's* crew had taken to a liferaft, but were soon picked up by the *Cape Carter.* Over 500 bales of contraband that had been ditched in the water were also recovered. There were so many bales that one of the helicopters used the wind force from its rotors to corral them.

Clean-up lasted all day, while helicopters ferried SWAT teams to suspected hiding places and brought back prisoners. Sixteen people in all were taken into custody, and their ship, trailer truck, and *three* ducks were seized. More than three tons of Thai sticks, a form of marijuana, were also recovered—with a street value of several million dollars.

And everybody but the smugglers went home to celebrate New Year's Eve.

Hundreds of millions of dollars worth of illegal drugs, brought into the country by sea, have been seized by the Coast Guard in joint operations like this one or in less complex captures.

Smuggling operations usually involve small craft which operate from a large "mother" ship lying outside the twelve-mile limit. Mother ships have been used for smuggling since colonial times, but then the ships lay close to shore. During Prohibition, rum runners, smuggling liquor, unloaded their contraband outside the twelve-mile limit, moving freely in their reliance on the age-old principle of freedom of the seas.

However, the 1958 Convention on the High Seas restricted that freedom. Even if a ship is outside a country's custom zone (in the case of the United States, twelve miles), it is subject to boarding and holding if it can be proved that she is a mother ship to vessels breaking the law within the custom zone. The Coast Guard still considers such boarding diplomatically sensitive, however, and always requests Washington to obtain permission of the country in which the ship is registered before it boards on the high seas.

As some states legalize limited use of marijuana, the Coast Guard feels their job will get bigger, not smaller. More

5

An overturned pleasure boatman is pulled from
the water with the aid of a life ring and the
crewman of a 44-foot motor lifeboat.

marijuana will be used, but because it is still a federal crime to bring it into the country, smuggling will undoubtedly increase.

The Coast Guard is not only concerned with the age-old problem of smuggling, but also with the equally old problem of piracy. Yes, pirates are still with us and, in fact, seem to be flourishing, particularly in Florida waters. They board small boats, steal money and jewels, and often the boats as well. Sometimes they murder passengers and crew.

Pirates, smugglers—the years have not civilized the seas overly much.

*Rescuing flood refugees is one of the many jobs performed by the U.S. Coast Guard.*

## SEA RAIDS AND RESCUES

The United States Coast Guard is the country's seagoing police force, working to bring law and order and help on the waters of our part of the world.

It has held that job since it was born as the Revenue Cutter Service in 1789 to stop smuggling—a way of life in the brand new country, the United States of America.

# 2

# "A SYSTEM OF CUTTERS . . ."

When John Hancock signed the Declaration of Independence "so big the King can read it without his glasses," he was waiting to be tried on several hundred counts of smuggling. So was his compatriot and cosigner, Samuel Adams. Smuggling, in fact, was the patriotic duty of all good American colonists who were not about to give King George III any tax money without representation in Parliament or, for that matter, with representation. Smuggling was a game every gentleman played, and when war finally came, it was a necessity.

But then the war was over, and the Americans had their own government—a representative, democratic government. It was 1789. George Washington had just stood on the balcony of the Treasury Building in New York, the country's new capital, and had been sworn in as president of a republic that was virtually bankrupt. The government needed money to pay the debts of war, to accomplish the goals for which the war had been fought, to grow, to protect itself, and to show that it could stand as a nation among other nations of the world. Otherwise it would soon be gobbled up again.

Where was the money to come from? The answer came quickly and easily: from duties on imports. The colonies,

9

strung out along the Atlantic seaboard, did almost all of their trading—foreign and domestic—by ship. Duties could be quickly imposed, since the mechanism for their collection remained from pre-Revolutionary days. And the duties would be lucrative.

As one of its first jobs, the new Congress somehow managed to stop disagreeing long enough to act on the matter, but it took four separate bills. A schedule of duties was drawn up, 59 legal ports of entry were designated, with collectors of revenue at each port. A Treasury Department was created by the Organic Act of 1789, which is still in force. For many years the Treasury Department was the most important and power-ful of the federal departments because Congress gave it so many duties: "to receive, keep, and disburse the monies of the United States"; to collect customs duties and excise taxes; to run the Lighthouse Service; to set up aids to navigation; to provide medical care for seamen; and even—for a short while—to run the mails.

Washington made a brilliant choice for his Secretary of the Treasury, a man he admired and trusted. His young friend had been on the newly-sworn president's staff throughout the war, had been a hero at the Battle of Yorktown, and had become an eminent lawyer and economist: Alexander Hamilton.

Hamilton swiftly outlined a master plan for making the United States a respected, responsible nation capable of paying its debts. It was a plan based largely on the income from the customs duties. These had been set high enough to place a burden on foreign states, including Rhode Island and North Carolina, who had yet to ratify the Constitution. But the duties were low enough to discourage smuggling, or so it was hoped.

Except that it didn't work that way. It did bring Rhode Island and North Carolina kicking and screaming into the fold to avoid the higher taxes, but it didn't bring much money into the Treasury. Independent Americans didn't like import taxes with a representative government any better than they had as British subjects, and so smuggling remained fair game. Coastal shipping between states was not taxed. It was an easy matter to off-load cargoes at sea into small boats that plied the coastal ports, or ships pulled into any of hundreds of deserted harbors and out-of-the-way anchorages known from colonial days.

Hamilton was not about to see his plans scuttled, and it didn't take him long to deal with that game. After consulting with customs collectors, he asked Congress to authorize the building of "a system of cutters" for patrol purposes. Congress quickly agreed, and on August 4, 1790, appropriated $10,000 for ten armed sloops and schooners.

Hamilton's "system of cutters" wasn't given an official name. Instead, it was referred to either as just "the revenue cutters," or "the Revenue Marine." But the 1790 birthdate of this fleet without a name is considered the birthdate of today's United States Coast Guard.

Alexander Hamilton wrote to the customs collectors of those districts under whose supervision the cutters were to serve, authorizing them to build their own cutters—with certain stringent provisions:

> *From my inquiries in the Port of New York, I find that a complete vessel, capable of keeping the Coast in the winter season, may be fitted for one thousand dollars, which sum you are not to exceed . . .*

Even in those days, $1,000 wasn't much money for an armed ship, but somehow they were built and outfitted. The *General Greene,* named after the Pennsylvania War hero Nathanael Greene, had a figurehead and decorations carved by the foremost master of the art in America, William Rush, at a cost of $35.67.

11

Officers for the revenue cutters were appointed by President Washington himself, with Hamilton's recommendation. Master's pay was $30 a month, and the pay scale went down from there to $4 a month for ship's boys. Rations were added: "rum, brandy or whisky 1 quart; 1 quart salt; 2 quarts vinegar; 2 pounds soap; 1 pound candles." It is no wonder that maintaining crews and ships cost the government only $23,327 a year!

They earned their keep hundreds of times over. The cutters were directly responsible for keeping the country solvent and respected. In less than two years, they collected over $4,300,000; by 1815, $24,000,000.

Their contribution was not only financial. This tiny fleet was also the only one the country had for defense. The Navy had been disbanded at the end of the Revolutionary War and was not reactivated until 1794. Its ships were not in service until 1797.

The task of defense was far too great for schooners and sloops. The Americans had many problems on the seas. Off Africa's Barbary Coast, pirates were demanding tribute and ransoms for American ships and the seamen they captured. Some Americans had spent up to ten years in Algerian prisons or chained to the thwarts of war galleys. Then, in 1801, Tripoli declared war on the United States and demanded one-fifth of all the country's resources—as tribute.

An undeclared war had also broken out between France and America, two former allies. The French, like Americans, had also revolted against a monarchy, and they expected American support in their growing enmity with Great Britain. Instead, the Americans were patching up their differences with their former mother country. Angered, the French sent hundreds of privateers to prey on American shipping, hoping to ruin the country financially and show up its weakness on the seas. Over 340 American merchant ships were captured.

A strong Navy was essential. And to add extra strength to

the newborn service, President John Adams directed that the revenue cutters be temporarily transferred to the Navy. It was an arrangement that the Congress made legal in a resolution that stands today, that "the Revenue Cutters shall, whenever the President of the United States so directs, cooperate with the Navy of the United States."

The cutters went on their first convoy duty, protecting merchant ships against French and Barbary pirates. They made 16 of the 20 captures of French ships and took back many captured American vessels.

One of the most famous engagements of this undeclared war with the French was the battle of the *Pickering* and *L'Egypte Conquise* on October 18, 1799. Outgunned and outmanned almost four to one, the *Pickering* fought the *Conquise* for nine murderous hours, until the French ship surrendered—an amazing victory for the tiny revenue cutter.

The *Pickering* and its crew had another fate in store for them than death at the hands of the French. A violent storm swept them into oblivion not long after their historic victory.

By 1801, the quasi-war with the French, which had been a matter of misguided politics since its beginning, had been resolved by diplomats. Magically, France was no longer the enemy. Great Britain was.

The rise of Napoleon was changing the balance of power in Europe, causing enmity between France and Britain until war was declared in 1803. Great Britian saw fit to replenish her ship's crews by impressing American seamen, claiming they were really British naval deserters or even British subjects because they had been British-born. This, of course, applied to a great many Americans in those days.

Outright war was delayed for many years, and then, when it seemed as if war could be avoided, there it was: the War of 1812. The Navy consisted of mostly gunboats, which President Jefferson favored for their mobility, but which had a hard time against the much larger British ships. But the Navy and the revenue cutters—then sixteen of them—did battle with the enemy and with privateers and did convoy duty as well. Nine cutters took 14 British ships. But not all their encounters were victorious.

The cutter *Surveyor,* with fifteen men, met HMS *Narcissus* in the York River on the night of June 12, 1813, in dense fog. The men fought as well as they could against superior guns and manpower but were finally forced to surrender. The next day the *Surveyor's* captain received the following communication:

HIS MAJESTY'S SHIP *Narcissus*

June 13, 1813

Sir: Your gallant and desperate attempt to defend your vessel against more than double your number, on the night of the 12th inst., excited such admiration on the part of your opponents, as I have seldom · witnessed, and induces me to return to you the sword you had so nobly used, in testimony of mine. Our poor fellows have severely suffered occasioned chiefly, if not solely, by the precautions you had taken to prevent suprise; in short, I am at a loss which to admire most, the arrangement on board the *Surveyor,* or the determined manner by which her deck was disputed, inch by inch.

You have my most sincere wishes for the immediate parole and speedy exchange of yourself and brave crew; and I cannot but regret, that I myself have no influence that way, otherwise it should be forthcoming.

14

I am, sir, with much respect,

Your most obedient,
John Crerie

Captain S. Travis
U.S. Cutter *Surveyor*

The revenue cutter *Eagle* was another casualty of the War of 1812, but not before her crew had put up an epic battle. The British brig *Despatch* was shepherding a group of barges and tenders which were preying on shipping in the Long Island Sound. The *Eagle* received word that the American sloop *Susan* was missing, probably the victim of one of the *Despatch*'s group. The *Eagle* set out to find the sloop, and find her they did—along with the *Despatch,* which, with 18 guns, was no match for the *Eagle.* There was no way to run, and the wind had died. Her best chance lay in beaching and taking up positions on a bluff on the south shore of the sound. After beaching her, the crew dragged her four small cannon up the bluff and set them up to return the *Despatch*'s fire. From this vantage point, they were able to hold off the British, but their ship was being badly pounded and her masts shot down.

The wadding for the cannon was running low. The *Eagle*'s captain asked for volunteers to leave their sheltered position on the cliff and climb aboard the *Eagle,* in full view of the British, to retrieve anything on board they could use for wadding. Each man in the entire crew volunteered. Five men were chosen by the captain, but only four lived to make it to the ship. They gathered up all the available cloth and the ship's log, as a full broadside of gunfire raked them. Undaunted, they pried the metal from the broadside out of the wooden hull to send back to the British when they reached their emplacements. And, as a parting gesture, they ran up a new ensign to replace the original, torn away by gunshot.

15

Under covering gunfire from the bluff, the four darted back, bent low. But they lost another man to the British guns.

British marines had gathered at the rails of the *Despatch* and were fixing bayonets for a charge up the bluff. But hurriedly distributing the wadding (including the pages of the log), the Americans set up a deadly accurate cannon barrage. The British made no landing that day. The *Despatch* sailed off, and the Americans returned to the *Eagle*, managing to refloat her. Sorely wounded, she tried to make a safe harbor the following morning but was easily captured by the *Despatch* lying in wait for her.

The battle had been won and lost, and even the history books have forgotten the names of the men who had fought so gallantly. But the name of the *Eagle* is memorialized by the three-masted sailing ship of the Coast Guard Academy, whose cadets train on her. The great days of sailing ships will not be forgotten by the men who carry on their tradition.

The War of 1812 finally drew to a close, and America's place among the nations of the world would never again be taken lightly.

The revenue cutters returned to their peacetime labors of guarding against smuggling and to a new duty: preserving quarantine of ships entering or leaving ports with yellow fever, a scourge of the 1800s. Another scourge of the era, the slave trade, had been made illegal, and the cutters sought out ships engaging in illicit transportation of slaves, capturing a number and setting their captives free.

The cutters' peacetime duties were shortly to be curtailed again by the pirates of the Spanish Main and the Seminole Wars.

Outlaws of the sea, with little or no regard for human life, these pirates preyed on shipping in the Gulf of Mexico, off the coasts of Florida and Georgia, and in the Caribbean. They plundered, burned, and murdered on land as well as on the seas. The United States was dependent for its survival on its

*A U.S. Revenue cutter near a ship in distress.*

foreign trade, and these depredations could not be allowed to continue. The revenue cutters were summoned into service.

Jean Lafarge, a lieutenant of the notorious Lafitte brothers, Jean (hero of the Battle of New Orleans) and Alexander, was in command of a Mexican privateer, the *Bravo,* that was ravaging shipping in the Gulf of Mexico. Two revenue cutters overtook and captured the *Bravo,* then destroyed the notorious Patterson's Town, a pirate city on an inlet of the Gulf. It was a death blow to piracy in the Gulf.

A number of privateers were captured by the revenue cutter *Active* in Chesapeake Bay, and the *Dallas* captured more off Savannah, Georgia. The British joined the fight against piracy in the waters off their possessions in the West Indies. When British and United States warships and the revenue cutter *Louisiana* took five pirate ships in 1822, the heyday of the buccaneer was over.

The revenue cutters fought beside the Army, as well as the Navy, in the Seminole Wars. The Seminoles were a branch of the Creek tribe who broke away and settled in Florida with a small group of Apalachee. They were joined by runaway slaves, and their numbers grew. Florida was then under Spanish rule, when the Spaniards paid attention, which was not often. They had only three settlements in Florida.

There was border scuffling when Americans crossed from Alabama and Georgia into Florida to hunt for runaway slaves. Some British traders added fuel to the fire whenever they could. A number of settlers on the American side were scalped, and a detachment of 40 soldiers were killed. Andy Jackson took a force of Tennessee militia and, under federal government orders, illegally crossed the Florida border and hauled down the colors of a Spanish settlement. Jackson had two Seminole chiefs and two British traders hung. Then he chased the Seminoles through the swamps toward Pensacola, the second of the three Spanish settlements. He ousted the Spanish governor and claimed the fort for the United States.

18

This did not make anybody happy. Back in Washington, there were threats of a court-martial. In England, there was a hue and cry for reparations for the death of the traders—or war. And in Spain, there was the realization that the time had come to get out of Florida while it could still be sold, otherwise it probably would be taken from the Spanish for nothing. After all, one settlement, in southern Florida, St. Augustine, was all Spain had left. So, on February 22, 1819, Spain sold all her lands east of the Mississippi and her claim to the Oregon country to the United States for $5,000,000. The British backed off diplomatically. And Andy Jackson escaped court-martial and eventually became President.

But the Seminoles' problem had not been solved. A treaty agreeing to repatriation on lands west of the Mississippi was signed by some of the Seminole leaders. But one chief, Osceola, refused to accept the treaty and killed the governor of Florida and four of his aides. On the same day, an Army column was attacked, and 108 men were killed. The Second Seminole War had started.

The guerilla tactics of the Seminoles, who made quick hit-and-run raids, were highly successful for a while. Then, eight revenue cutters were ordered into Florida waters, transporting troops and equipment—the first amphibious landings with combined forces in American history. Now the tide was turned against the Seminoles, with the power of men and money on the government's side. And the Army took a lesson in warfare from the Indians which proved even more effective than numbers of men and dollars: they burned crops and destroyed villages in quick, systematic raiding.

With winter coming, the Seminoles could not survive without food and shelter, and they finally agreed to repatriation.

The war was over. It had lasted eight years, from 1835 to 1843. It had cost the United States more than $20,000,000 and the lives of over 1,500 military men. No one knows how many

Seminole lives were lost, but they had lost their homes and their land.

While the revenue cutters were engaged in their military role, they received orders that added a different dimension to their duties. In 1836, the cutters were ordered "to aid persons at sea, in distress, who may be taken aboard," and, in 1843, "to preserve properties and cargoes from wrecks for the owners."

Because the revenue cutters were playing many roles, they needed a manager to get it all together. And they got one, a bureau all their own called the Revenue Marine Bureau, with its own operating staff, personnel department, and director. Now they had a name, although still not an official one: the Revenue Marine.

But before long, the revenue cutters were back in the Navy. The United States was at war again, this time with Mexico.

The revenue cutters emerged forward from this war covered with glory. In fact, they barely made it into the fighting. The ships were either too old, or, if they were new, they were steam-propelled—and a headache to one and all. The *Polk* leaked so badly on launching that it never went into service. Another cutter, on her way to the war, sprung a leak and had to be beached. Two others were so unseaworthy they were turned into lightships. Since salt water was used in square boilers to make their steam, it is really a wonder that they all didn't simply blow up.

The *Harriet Lane,* named after President Buchanan's niece, was the Revenue Marine's first successful steam cutter. She was to have quite a career. Shortly after she was launched, the *Harriet Lane* was sent to Paraguay to enforce a trade agreement there. The United States was learning gunboat diplomacy.

Soon, the country was experiencing the horrors of the Civil War. The election of Lincoln to the presidency had started a wave of antifederalism throughout the South. The Confederate flag flew over lighthouses, customs houses, and some revenue cutters by Inauguration Day. And on April 12, 1861, the shooting war started at Fort Sumter in Charleston Harbor. The *Harriet Lane,* sent as part of a naval squadron to relieve the Fort, is credited with firing the first shot of the war on the seas, when she challenged and held the steamer *Nashville* with a shot across the bow. She was also part of the first naval victory for the Union: the capture of Fort Clark and Fort Hatteras in North Carolina, bases for blockade runners.

But the *Harriet Lane* was soon to change sides. When she was part of the Union blockade of Galveston Harbor, to stop the shipment of cotton in exchange for war supplies, she was boarded by Confederates. After a bloody hand-to-hand combat, the *Harriet Lane* was captured. She spent the rest of the war as a Confederate gunboat.

The revenue cutter *Miami* made history, also. One dark spring night early in the war, she landed Abraham Lincoln in Confederate territory outside the city of Norfolk, Virginia, where Union forces were bogged down. Accompanied by his Secretary of War, Edwin Stanton, and Salmon P. Chase, his Secretary of Treasury and head of the Revenue Marine, Lincoln conferred with the commander of the Union forces in Virginia, General Egbert Viele. Lincoln decided that an assault on Norfolk was in order, and the assault was carried out victoriously the next day.

One cutter that turned Confederate, the *Clarence,* raided Union ships off Virginia, burning three and capturing three others. *Clarence*'s commander, Lt. Charles W. Read, sailed off on one of the Yankee ships, the *Tacony,* all the way to Portland, Maine, burning and capturing at least a dozen more ships in his guise as a Yankee. Switching to still another ship in case word of the *Tacony*'s deception had gone before him, he had it disguised as a fishing boat and his men as fishermen. Read sailed under the guns of the forts at Portland and right by the revenue cutter *Caleb Cushing*. Anchoring, Read sent small groups of men ashore to casually stroll the streets until they met and set fire to two ships under construction and all the city's wharves. Somehow, the fire didn't take hold. But Lt. Read was a most resourceful man. He had learned on his stroll through the city that the captain of the *Caleb Cushing* had died of a heart attack just a few hours before. Without a commander, the *Cushing* would be easy prey.

Read and his men waited for the moon to set. In small boats they made their way to the *Cushing* and boarded her. The surprised cuttermen were quickly overpowered. There was a quick raising of sails, and Read and his men were out of the harbor before the forts realized what had happened. But then the wind died. The ship would not move. The ever-quick lieutenant set two of his small boats to towlines and boldly towed the *Caleb Cushing* out to sea to catch the wind. They almost made it.

But by this time, the Portland Collector of Customs, responsible for the *Caleb Cushing* in peace time, finally realized what was going on and hurriedly organized a chase. The pursuers finally caught up with the *Cushing* ten miles out, capturing it and the daring lieutenant.

Finally, the bitter war was over. The dead were mourned on both sides, and the living breathed a silent prayer that they had somehow made it through the long dark time. On April 27, 1865, eighteen days after Lee's surrender at Appomattox Courthouse, some 2,000 Yankees, released from prisoner of war camps in the South, boarded the steamer *Sultana* in Memphis, Tennessee, for the voyage north on the Mississippi to Cairo, Illinois. They were finally going home after long years of horror. But there was more horror before them, and most would never see their homes.

During the night, the *Sultana*'s boiler exploded, and the ship went up in flames. Those who did not die in the explosion and fire jumped into the black river, icy from spring runoffs, to drown. Those who managed to reach the river's bank died of exposure before help could reach them.

About 1,500 people died that night. The *Sultana* was authorized to carry only 376 passengers. It was possible that the pressure in her boilers had been raised beyond their capacity, to move upstream a ship loaded to almost ten times its capacity in human cargo.

It was time to reactivate the regulations of the Steamboat Inspection Service, another of the ancestors of today's Coast Guard.

# 3

# THE STEAMBOAT
# INSPECTION SERVICE

Contrary to our textbooks, Robert Fulton did *not* invent the steamboat. But he was the first to build a successful commercial steamboat, in 1807. Just how successful these first steamers were is debatable. One of every eight blew up. In April 1838, the Mississippi steamboat *Oronoko* blew, killing over 100 people. A few days later, on the Ohio, the *Moselle* went up, with some 200 passenger and crew lives cost.

Clearly, something had to be done to insure the safety of these ships and their passengers. Some states tried to set standards of operation, but most river traffic crossed state lines, and a single state's regulations had little meaning. The federal government refused to take on the responsibility. It would constitute interference in private enterprise, they said. And anyway, went the reasoning, shipowners, who stood to lose the most from a sinking, were the best motivated to see to the safety of their ships, and they were best left to police themselves.

This policy of noninterference was not working—a fact finally recognized when still another passenger ship exploded with another large loss of life. Congress finally reacted to public outrage, and in July, 1838, it passed a steamboat inspection bill.

It wasn't much of a law, but it recognized the need for the regular inspection of hulls and boilers, for lifeboats and firefighting equipment, and for certificates of inspection to show that all standards had been met. But the law was limited to those ships carrying passengers. Crews were considered to have signed on at their own risk, so no safety provisions need apply to them! This was true even of crews on passenger ships, for whom no lifeboat spaces were provided until well into the twentieth century.

Another serious flaw in this first steamboat inspection law was that it provided for inspectors to be appointed by federal judges. Because federal judges were not the best judges of steamboat inspectors, many unqualified men were given the jobs, and so the job did not get done.

The steamships kept blowing up. The first eight months of 1852 saw seven major disasters, costing nearly 700 lives. The government tried again, this time organizing a Steamboat Inspection Service to report to the Secretary of the Treasury, as the Revenue Marine Bureau did. Local authorities were to administer the inspection laws, and a central board of inspectors was appointed as a supervisory body. Additional safety measures and trained, licensed engineers and pilots were required on passenger ships.

There was some improvement in disaster statistics, but not enough. Then the great disaster of them all befell the country—the Civil War—and rules and regulations about safety went out the window. When the master of the *Sultana* packed some 2,000 people in a ship whose Certificate of Inspection allowed less than 400, he was responding to careless wartime habits. And when he had a damaged boiler plate replaced with a patch of thinner metal almost guaranteed to blow out, he was acting with the same irresponsibility to which war had accustomed him.

In the postwar turmoil of Reconstruction, it took somewhat longer for Congress to respond to the *Sultana* disaster. Not until February, 1871, did a new steamboat inspection act reorganize the Service, stiffening its safety provisions. This time the law was extended to include all ships above a certain size, whether they carried passengers or not, and to all persons, passengers and crew members alike. Masters and chief mates became subject to licensing. Incredibly, they had not been required to show proof of competency before this.

Postwar trade was booming. More and more steamships plied the rivers and the oceans, bringing goods and people from Europe and from the cities of the East to the frontiers of the West. More ships brought about more wrecks. And every time one of the steamships foundered, there was a public outcry against the Steamboat Inspection Service. The fact that the Service might request improvements in safety regulations for years on end without being heard by an indifferent Congress did not matter when the public was aroused. The Service was the whipping boy.

Then, on June 15, 1904, one of the greatest marine disasters of all time took place on New York City's East River. The wooden paddle-wheel excursion steamer *General Slocum,* with 740 children and 640 adults on board for a day's outing, caught fire. For some reason, the captain kept the ship going into the wind at normal speed. As thousands watched from onshore, frantic passengers jumped overboard. Many were caught in the great slicing blades of the paddle wheel. The lifeboats were tied down by wires which could not be loosened or cut, the water pumps failed, and the life jackets were largely unusable—they had not been inspected for ten years. The crew ignored the plight of the passengers and fought their way to safety. Only one crewman died, of drowning, his body weighted down with money he had looted. A total of 1,030 passengers died. Over 500 were children.

President Theodore Roosevelt himself ordered an investigation and the firing of all Steamboat Service officers involved in the disaster. Whether they all deserved this "whipping" is not clear, but unquestionably many did.

Then Congress instituted more laws for safety, most of which had been recommended by the Service ten or twenty years before.

It took the greatest marine disaster of them all, the sinking of the *Titanic* on April 15, 1912, to bring about a change in safety regulations so simple it seems incredible that no one had thought about it before: enough lifeboat spaces for every person on board a ship. Approximatly 1,500 people—the exact number will probably never be known—died that night when the supposedly unsinkable ship struck an iceberg. She stayed afloat for 2½ hours, long enough for everyone to have gotten off her safely *if* there had been enough lifeboats. She carried sixteen lifeboats and four collapsible boats, with a total carrying capacity of 1,167 people. She had 2,208 people on board. When the *Titanic* was outfitted, her British owners provided every conceivable convenience, every possible luxury, and double the number of lifeboats required by law. But the laws governing lifeboats had not been changed in Great Britain since the days of the small steam packets. Doubling an indequate number of lifeboats was not adequate. And no one thought to count heads.

But even with 1,167 lifeboat spaces, only 703 people filled them. Another 42 men, who went down with the *Titanic,* saved themselves by clinging to an overturned lifeboat or managed to get into a half-submerged collapsible boat. Many lifeboats had gone off half loaded and, fearful of being swamped, they did not pick up survivors in the water. Although there was no panic and plenty of time, passengers and many of the crew simply did not know how to handle the lifeboat evacuation.

Some of the wealthiest and most famous families in America had members on the *Titanic.* The public knew their

*A Coast Guard-manned frigate maneuvers to tow
a blazing liner away from a town in Alaska.*

names, fantasized their lives, and felt close to them. Their
tragic fate stirred the country into an uproar—far more than
the equally tragic fates of the hundreds of immigrants aboard
who had scrimped and saved for third-class passage.

Again the public's demand for action brought forth new
protective regulations: lifeboat spaces for all, lifeboat drills,
and crewmen on board with special certification for manning
lifeboats. And a revenue cutter was sent to patrol the North
Atlantic shipping lanes to guard against the threat of wander-
ing icebergs.

An International Convention of Safety of Life at Sea was convened in London in 1914 to pool the knowledge of many countries and to make the recommendations necessary for safety on the seas. The convention requested that the patrol undertaken by the Revenue Cutter Service be made permanent, its expenses to be paid in proportionate shares by the countries whose ships would be protected. Thus, the International Ice Patrol was born, and the Revenue Cutter Service's humanitarian, lifesaving mission was given equal emphasis with its law-enforcement duties.

# 4

# THE BERING SEA PATROL

The revenue cutters were no strangers to service in the ice-bound waters of the far North. Soon after Secretary of State William Henry Seward negotiated the purchase of Russian America—Alaska—in 1867, the Revenue Cutter Service started patrolling the area. They were practically the only government the area had. They apprehended criminals, enforced the law, and made up "floating courts." They gathered military intelligence for the Navy, carried the mail for the Post Office Department, brought in teachers and missionaries, checked up on sanitation, guarded timber and game, carried Public Health Service doctors and nurses, and performed marriages—a privilege reserved to the cutters' masters.

One of the most famous of the Revenue Cutter masters was Captain Michael A. Healy, who went to Alaskan waters in 1868 on the Bering Sea Patrol. He was the son of an Irish immigrant who became a wealthy southern planter in Georgia and married a slave.

"Cap'n Mike" Healy became a legend in his own time. At the end of his tour in Alaskan waters, the *New York Sun* carried an article about Healy, calling him

31

. . . a good deal more distinguished person in the
waters of the far Northwest than any president of
the United States or any potentate of Europe has
yet become. He stands for law and order in many
thousand square miles of land and water, and if
you should ask in the Arctic Sea, 'Who is the
greatest man in America?' the instant answer
would be, 'Why, Mike Healy. . . . he's the
United States.' He holds in these parts a power
of attorney for the whole country.

In 1886, Healy took command of a ship that was to
become as much of a legend as he was, the revenue cutter
*Bear*. Before joining the Revenue Cutter Service, *Bear* had
been built as a sealer. She served as a Navy ship, one of three
searching for the lost members of the Lady Franklin Bay
Expedition in the Arctic.

The *Bear* and two other cutters were the Bering Sea
Patrol, with Mike Healy in command. One of their first jobs
was to stop seal poaching in the Bering Sea. In the first year of
patrol, twelve Canadian schooners were captured as poachers.
And Healy's fleet went on capturing Canadian poachers until
the United States and Great Britain were at the point of war in
1892. Britain maintained that the captures were made outside
of the three-mile limit of the United States' jurisdiction, and
that seals, as wild animals, were lawful prey to one and all.
The United States position was that the entire Bering Sea was
under her control as once it had been under Russian control,
that jurisdiction having been passed on to the United States
when Alaska was sold. And besides, no mater what, the
slaughter of seals could not and would not continue.

The matter finally had to be turned over to international
arbitration, and the United States lost.

But Captain Healy and his fleet continued to do what they
could to protect the seals and to convoy them on their annual

migrations. Still, the massacre of seals went on until a treaty was signed in 1911 between the United States, Great Britain, Russia, and Japan. The treaty prohibited seal hunting by anyone except the natives, who were allowed to hunt with their more primitive weapons. They were not allowed to use repeating rifles.

When the *Bear* made its annual spring visit to the Eskimos on King Island, Healy found them starving, barely able to walk; 200 of the island's population of 300 had died of starvation. The walrus, their main food supply, had not come that fall. And their way to the mainland had been blocked by unusually severe winter storms.

The food supply of the Eskimos was being depleted by white hunters with modern equipment. They had also brought alcohol to the Eskimos, whose bodies were unused to this hard liquor. Soon, a good many of them became addicted and were unable to hunt or provide food.

Healy was determined to help. He and Dr. Sheldon Jackson, a missionary, hit upon the idea of importing reindeer from a group of Siberian natives called Tchuktchi. Reindeer could be herded and bred like cattle, and they provided milk, meat, and skins for the Eskimos.

It was an inspired plan with almost insurmountable obstacles. The Tchuktchi were superstitious about selling their animals. And if they could finally be convinced to sell, there was the problem of transporting the reindeer across the Bering Sea. If the revenue cutters could bring the animals across, would the United States be willing to pay the costs? And if everything else was accomplished, would the Eskimos be willing to turn from hunters to herdsmen?

Somehow, Healy and Jackson got it all to work. The Tchuktchi sold the reindeer, the government paid, and the revenue cutters transported. The Eskimos were trained in reindeer culture at the government and mission schools and were given pairs of reindeer to breed to develop their own

33

herds. A hunting culture was turned to a herding one, and the Alaskan Eskimo was saved from extinction.

Healy's career was to end under a cloud, his sometimes strong-minded disciplinary actions challenged by his officers. But the *Bear* went on to even more glory.

In 1897, a fleet of whaling ships was trapped when an unexpectedly early winter froze them in. It would be July or August before the polar pack ice would open sufficiently to let the ships out, that is, if they had not been crushed by the battering force of pack ice against their hulls. The almost 300-man crews could not hope to survive unless supplies could be brought to them.

The *Bear* was chosen to go to their rescue, with a volunteer crew aboard. But the closest the *Bear* could get to the whalers was 2,000 miles. Three Revenue Service officers, Lt. David Jarvis, 2nd Lt. E.P. Bertholf (who was to become a commandant of the Coast Guard), and the ship's doctor, S.J. Call, went after the men by dog team. It was bitter cold, often dipping to 70° below zero. Wild winds and driving snow lashed at them as they kept up an unmerciful pace over mountains and tundra. They went across the huge ice expanse of Kotzebue Sound, struggling always against an enemy even worse than the weather—time.

The men picked up two herds of reindeer along the way from a native and from the U.S. government reindeer station at Cape Barrow, 700 miles from the trapped men. The reindeer would provide the food they would need until the rescuers and rescued could move out.

The Overland Expedition, as it was called in the newspapers, had started out in mid-December 1897. They reached their goal on March 29, 1898, after 3½ months of torturous travel. They found the whalers near death from disease and near crazed from the seemingly hopelessness of their situation; a few were reduced to bestiality. Food and medicine were quickly distributed, housing was constructed, sanitary rules

*The Coast Guard's newest and largest icebreaker,*
Polar Sea.

were laid down, inspections were held, and the herds were
tended—military discipline imposed to keep the men alive and
sane until the *Bear* could reach them. They had to wait until
the end of July before the ice opened enough for the *Bear* to
make it. She carried in provisions for the whaling ships that
could still sail and brought out the crews whose ships had been
destroyed by the pack ice. The Overland Expedition had
achieved a miraculous rescue. The men went home to great,
but fleeting, fame.

The *Bear* served on the grueling Bering Sea Patrol for a

*The U.S. Coast Guard's* Polar Star.

total of 41 years, an incredible span of time. But still more adventures lay ahead of her. She carried Admiral Richard Byrd to the Antarctic, and she fought in World War II as part of the rigorous Greenland Patrol. The *Bear* was 90 when she died. She was being towed to Philadelphia to become a floating restaurant, a shoddy end for the proud old ship, when a storm arose. She broke in two and sank to a more fitting ending than the one that had been planned for her.

The exploits of that one great ship were the embodiment of all the missions of the Revenue Cutter Service—military, police, judicial, and lifesaving—typifying the proud heritage of today's United States Coast Guard.

# 5

# THE LIFESAVING
# SERVICE

Strange as it may seem to us today, concern for the saving of
lives at sea is a comparatively new concept. Crews of ships
were considered to be there at their own risk. They carried on
their missions, and their safety was their own concern. It
wasn't until passengers traveled on ships that there were any
stirrings toward safety considerations.

Beacons and lighthouses to guide ships to safety are
almost as old as civilization, the first dating back to ancient
Egypt where priests maintained the beacon fires. The lighthouse of Pharos, built in the third century B.C., functioned
for 1,500 years. It was lighted by a wood fire, its smoke a signal
by day, its glow a signal by night. The lights of these structures
were meant not as warnings of danger, but as guides to dark
harbors.

In America, colonization had been going on for over a
century before the first lighthouse was built, in 1716, on Little
Brewster Island in Boston harbor. (There may have been a
beacon light at the French stockade on the mouth of the
Mississippi somewhat earlier, but no one can document it for
certain until 1721.) A tonnage tax of one penny per ton on all
vessels moving in and out of the harbor, except coasters, paid
for the Boston Light.

The first keeper of the Boston Light was George Worthylake, whose name was most appropriate to his position but whose fate was not. Worthylake, his wife, his daughter, and two men were drowned when the lighthouse boat capsized on the way to the island. The young printer Benjamin Franklin wrote a ballad, "Lighthouse Tragedy," to commemorate the event and, as was the custom of the times, hawked it on the streets of the city.

The second keeper of the Boston Light, John Hayes, kept a seaman's hostel there until he was able to force the good leaders of Massachusetts Colony to give him a pay raise. He also asked for, and received, "a great gun (that) may be placed on said Island to answer ships in a Fogg."

When British troops occupied Boston in 1775, a small American detachment burned the wooden parts of the lighthouse. The British set about repairing it under guard, and Washington sent 300 men in whaleboats to stop them. They did so but were stopped in turn by British boats as they left the island. A fierce battle routed the British with heavy casualties, while the Americans lost only one man.

When the British finally left Boston in June, 1776, they reversed roles with the Americans. Now it was the British who tried to destroy the Boston Light. They succeeded with a time charge which blew it to smithereens. Not to be daunted, the Americans gathered up the pieces of iron that were once the top of the lighthouse and used them for cannon shot.

The Boston Light was rebuilt in 1783, and it stands to this day to safely guide mariners home.

In 1789, the new government of the United States took over the care of lighthouses. In 1852, the Lighthouse Board was established to supervise the construction of warning signals. The Lighthouse Board became the Lighthouse Service in 1910 and part of the United States Coast Guard in 1939.

Lighthouses and beacons slowly appeared along the coastline as more and more ships carrying cargoes and colonists arrived in the new country of the United States of America. But now people were showing more concern for the safety of these voyagers. Perhaps they remembered their own recent arrivals and their fears of stranding on sandbars all along the coast or of being blown away from their anchorage.

Once the wooden ships went aground, the ferocity of wind-whipped waves easily crushed their hulls or high winds keeled them over. There was nothing one could do for the people on board but pick them up if they made it to the beaches, and give them food and shelter if they were still alive. That is, if anyone was even aware that a wreck had occurred. Sometimes, only a beachcomber coming by after a storm might find some wreckage or a body to testify to a wreck that no one knew had happened.

In 1806, the government appointed a Coast Survey to chart the country's shoreline to make navigation safer. But it was still up to private groups to provide what relief they could to the shipwrecked.

The Massachusetts Humane Society, organized in the late 1700s by a group of concerned private citizens, was a leader in attempts to help the shipwrecked. The citizens built numerous small huts in protected spots along the coast to be used as shelters. The houses were stocked with rockets for sending signal flares, with straw and matches for building fires in the tiny fireplaces, with dry biscuits for food, and with donated clothing. However, for a shipwreck victim to find a hut was chancy. The Society printed pamphlets giving directions to each of the huts and distributed them on ocean-going vessels. Exactly how they expected some shipwrecked, half-drowned soul to salvage a pamphlet, read it in the darkness of a storm or night, and drag himself or herself a mile or so across some devious route to reach a hut is difficult to understand. It is also not known how much these huts were used, but one must assume that the good citizens of Massachusetts would not have continued to build them if their use had not been effectively demonstrated. However, many of the shelters fell into disrepair, their meager supplies taken. The horror of a shipwreck victim, who thought help was on hand only to find ashes, is painful to contemplate.

The problems of shipwrecks were not only in relation to their human victims. There was also the large problem of salvage. In the earliest days of trading by sea, the wealth of a wrecked ship and its cargo belonged to whoever found them. This could be a very lucrative find. Ancient governments were quick to realize this and equally quick to claim their share of the wealth of salvage.

But it didn't take them much longer to realize that they were often the losers as well as the finders, and that other governments and people were living off the wealth of *their* ships. That's when they started setting out beacons to guide their people home and charted their waters to keep ships from danger. And that's when they formulated laws to govern the disposition of salvage so that it was not all a matter of finders-keepers.

The laws of salvage have not changed much over the centuries. Basically, they state that wrecked ships and cargoes still belong to their owners, just as they had when they were whole. Anyone rescuing this property after a wreck becomes an agent of the owner, entitled to payment by the owner for his efforts, either in money or by keeping a share of the salvage. And, of course, the governments saw to it that salvage laws included a provision of compensation for them.

From about the fifteenth century on, insurance was available to shipowners through marine underwriters who guaranteed payment to merchants should their ships and cargoes be lost. The insurance companies or underwriters, therefore, became the owners for purposes of salvage.

The American colonies were quick to set up laws of

salvage, which became part of the laws reserved to the states when the new country was formed. Certain officials, usually sheriffs, were appointed to take charge of salvage operations in their areas, to protect the interests of owners and of the state. These men were to become known as wreck-masters.

The wreck-masters, in turn, appointed an agent from among the local citizenry to work for them. Then the agent recruited groups of fishermen or experienced surfmen to do the actual work of salvage. These men were called salvors or wreckers. Their payment came from what the owners gave them. And—in the beginning, at least—they were under no legal or financial obligation to salvage people.

But the wreckers were generally respectable and responsible people who lived near the ocean because they loved it and made their living from it. Because many of them had lost some member of their families to the sea, they risked their lives to salvage what shipwrecked humanity they could, without any thought of payment.

Quite probably they kept bits of wreckage they could use for themselves, perhaps netting, cloth, rope, nails, and other things to make their meager existence a bit more comfortable. No one could blame them if they didn't turn everything over to the agents. But to accuse them of pilferage, as some did, was wrong. There was more respect for rights in those days than today. A piece of salvage washed onto beaches might bear a marker (a pattern of rocks or a cross of branches) to claim the salvor's rights, which were respected by all.

Not that there weren't cases of looting and pillaging of wrecks, but it was not by wreckers. Sometimes onlookers, sometimes even survivors, did the looting. On some sections of the coast there were pirates, who put out in small boats to steal from helpless passengers. There were also looters who placed false lights to wreck ships on their shores. They were known as "mooncussers," those who "cussed the moon" for shining because darkness was better for their murderous deeds.

Block Island, nine miles south of Rhode Island to which it belongs, was a famous rendezvous for pirates and looters. The *Palatine,* an emigrant ship from Holland on its way to Philadelphia, was driven far north by winds, to wreck on Block Island. Before any looters could get to them, however, the crew mutinied, killed their captain, and held up the passengers. Food supplies on board were sold at fantastic prices to passengers waiting to be rescued—or drowned. When the crew had stolen everything they could from the passengers, they took the boats and left. Wreckers finally got to the stranded ship and took off the passengers. But the story goes that one woman went mad and refused to leave the ship, even when it went on fire. The screams of the mad woman echoed over the waters as the blazing ship moved toward the current. The screams are said to echo still around Block Island's Palatine Lighthouse on the anniversary of the disaster.

There were other notorious groups of mooncussers along the coast. The town of Nags Head, North Carolina, is supposed to have gotten its name from the way its inhabitants attracted salvage to their shores. Horses, with lanterns slung around their necks, were walked along the beach. The lights bobbed rhythmically, looking exactly like the running lights of a ship. An unwary ship's captain would see the lights off toward the shore and think he had plenty of deep water to navigate in, only to find himself suddenly aground and at the mercy of the mooncussers.

In New Jersey, there were the "Barnegat Bay Pirates," and in Cape Cod and other Massachusetts inlets, there were other gangs of mooncussers. How much of their plundering and murdering was fact, and how much fiction, is unknown. Newspaper accounts had a tendency to lump legitimate wreckers together with pirates and mooncussers, so that all salvage activities were suspect.

The wreckers' work grew as more and more ships came to this country. In Massachusetts, the Humane Society was busier than ever caring for the increasing numbers of ship-wrecked victims. They were also responsible for setting up this country's first lifeboat station in 1807. The British had developed the first lifeboat and other pieces of lifesaving equipment, and the Massachusetts Humane Society kept in close contact with Britain's Royal National Lifeboat Institution, developing a good deal of their equipment cooperatively.

In New York and Philadelphia, other humane societies were forming to assist thousands of shipwrecked victims.

The 1830s saw the advent of the beautiful, swift Yankee clippers, with their clouds of sails that seemed to move the ships across the ocean with the speed of soaring seabirds. They were even faster than the early steam packets, which had the unfortunate habit of blowing up. The clippers brought hundreds of thousands of immigrants across the Atlantic to the New World—usually New York.

As ships approached New York harbor, they had to avoid the New Jersey offshore sandbars and low beaches to the west and south. Though not hard to do in fair weather, it was another matter in a storm or high winds. Driven up on the sandbars or unable to manipulate in a storm to avoid swamping, many ships came to a sorry end only a few hundred yards from the land their passengers had dreamed of reaching.

The American bark *Mexico* was not one of the new clipper ships. Consequently, she had spent some 60 days at sea with 112 seasick immigrants aboard. Now, finally, she had reached New York harbor. She lay up off Sandy Hook, New Jersey, the signal flags on her mast calling for a pilot. But it was a Sunday, a time when pilots did not work. As the *Mexico* waited, the weather turned bad, and high winds heralded a blizzard. The captain fought to keep the ship steady where she was and fired distress rockets for assistance. But the sea was too violent for even the most courageous of would-be rescuers. Slowly but surely, the *Mexico* lost her battle with the ever-heightening surf and blizzard winds. Helplessly, she was driven northeast, striking the shore of Long Island at what is now Long Beach. There were no survivors.

A reporter went to see where the ship had founded. He described how he found, laid out in a nearby barn, the bodies of "all ages and sexes . . . frozen and as solid as marble . . . in the very dresses in which they perished; . . . there were four or five beautiful little girls, from six to sixteen years of age, their cheeks and lips as red as roses, with their calm blue eyes open, looking at you in the face as if they could speak. I could hardly realize they were dead. I touched their cheeks and they were frozen as hard and solid as rock. . . ."

It was a scene to be repeated with many variations over the next decade. In 1844, the Austrian ship *Terasto* foundered off the New Jersey coast, wrecked on a sandbar. Dr. William A. Newell was making a call on a patient when the dreaded cry "ship ashore!" went up, and, hurrying to help, he found he could do nothing but stand by helplessly watching as all of the crew drowned.

But Dr. Newell didn't forget. In 1847, the doctor was elected to the House of Representatives in Washington. He asked Congress for help for the shipwrecked. No one listened. But a few months later, a lighthouse appropriation bill was being considered. Dr. Newell proposed an amendment to it, calling for further appropriation for

> . . . surfboats, rockets, carronades, and other necessary apparatus for the better protection of life and property from shipwrecks on the coast of New Jersey, between Sandy Hook and Little Egg Harbor, ten thousand dollars; the same to be expended under the supervision of such officers of the Revenue Marine Corps as may be detached for this duty by the Secretary of the Treasury.

44

*A patrolman of the U.S. Lifesaving Service sights a vessel in distress and burns a flare to indicate that help is coming.*

The bill and amendment were quickly passed, perhaps not so much on their merits but because it was August and Congress was anxious to get out of Washington. In any case, the organization that was later to be called the United States Lifesaving Service was born and given into the keeping of what was later to be called the Revenue Cutter Service. Both organizations were to become the United States Coast Guard.

Captain Douglas Ottinger was the man chosen by the Secretary of the Treasury to develop the lifesaving system. Together with advisors from the Board of Underwriters of New York, various marine insurance agents, and wreck masters, Ottinger chose eight locations for the building of lifesaving stations. These were simple, but sturdy, structures for housing the lifesaving equipment and for providing temporary shelter for the shipwrecked.

Sixteen more stations were soon added, so that each station was about ten miles apart. Each had a boat; a mortar with its lines, powder, and shot; a stove, fuel, and provisions; and blankets and clothes donated by humane societies. Each also had a cart for carrying the boat and other equipment to the water. The carts could be pulled by horses or by rescuers. Rescuers were generally recruited from among the wreckers, and they had as their leader a wreck-master. The stations had the advantage of being easily moved around as the beach changed shape from the action of surf and storms.

Ottinger didn't always take the advice he was given, notably in his insistence on iron lifeboats hated by the surfmen, who preferred their lighter, cedarwood boats. Ottinger favored the long-wearing, low-maintenance qualities of iron, but then he didn't have to drag the equipment for miles across dunes and snowdrifts and over rocks and sand.

The despised iron surfboats soon found their way into other things, such as pig-scalding or mixing mortar. They were not one of Ottinger's successes, but his eprouvette mortar was. Most wrecks were on sandbars about 300 to 400 yards

*A lifecar in operation on a line breeching ship and shore.*

offshore. It was not too long a haul for boats, but too often the lifeboats could not be launched because of the weather. What was needed was a sturdy line between ship and shore by which people could be brought off or assistance sent to them. But how could a line be sent out the necessary distance? The British had used a mortar successfully, but British wrecks were closer inshore, and the line didn't have to travel too far. Somehow the mortars had to be souped up for American use. But a larger powder charge always parted the line. Ottinger devised a kind of steel coil, or spring, which attached the line to the shot and prevented its parting. His eprouvette mortar achieved a range of well over 300 yards and was used for about 30 years until it was replaced by the Lyle gun with a range of over 400 yards.

Captain Ottinger also worked out a plan for a kind of enclosed gondola to ride on a hawser drawn between ship and shore. Passengers entered through a hatch on top, to be carried quickly and safely over and through the waves—perhaps with a bit of claustrophobia. He called the gondola a "surfcar." Ottinger gave his idea to Joseph Francis, who had produced the iron lifeboats, and, Francis actually turned it into a "lifecar" and claimed credit for its invention. The resultant feud between the two men clouded the very real achievement in lifesaving that the surfcar/lifecar made.

On January 12, 1850, just a short while after the surfcar was built, its use was very effectively demonstrated. The British ship *Ayrshire,* grounded on a sandbar during a north-easter, heeled over toward the beach, taking a terrible pounding from waves hitting her broadside. Passengers and crew huddled together in the small houses on deck or were lashed to the bulwarks and whatever rigging that was still standing. Water poured over them as huge waves hit their weather side. Freezing cold, wet, and terrified, they could see no sign of the storm abating and no hope of rescue. But, although they couldn't see it, there was a lifesaving station

*A breeches buoy, used by the U.S. Lifesaving
Service, the forerunner of the U.S. Coast Guard.*

close by. The station wasn't manned, but somehow the wreck was discovered, and help was fast in coming. The rescuers set up the brand new surfcar apparatus. Back and forth the surfcar went, carrying four people at a time, until all but one of the 202 persons aboard was brought to land. That one fatality was a man who insisted on accompanying his sister and her three daughters in the surfcar. Because there was no room for him inside, he leaped on the outside of the car and tried to hold on, but he was swept off by the surf.

Some of the English and Irish immigrants on the *Ayrshire* were so grateful to their rescuers that they chose to settle right there; some of their children eventually became lifesavers themselves.

The surfcar was to save many more lives of grateful immigrants and others. The breeches buoy, another British invention, also was used to bring people off wrecks. It was essentially a life ring with canvas cutoff pants, or breeches, suspended from it. The person stepped into the pants, held on to the ropes from which the buoy was hanging, and was whizzed away for what must have been a harrowing ride over or through the surf. Just exactly what women did with the billowing skirts they wore in the nineteenth century is not documented, but it is certainly hard to evision them fitting into a breeches buoy. However, the breeches buoy remained a valuable lifesaving tool well into the twentieth century, so it must have done its work well.

The early lifesavers did a magnificent job, especially considering that they were volunteers who rarely received rewards. They had no regulations to go by, no one to do maintenance or repairs on stations or equipment, and many, many bosses. They were subject to people like Captain Ottinger and his men, the Revenue Marine Bureau, the various private boards of underwriters who sometimes helped finance their work, the different humane societies, and the state salvage laws. Yet, when the cry "Ship Ashore!" was raised, they risked their lives and health.

It was hard to get money for equipment or for mainte-nance and repair from Congress. There were always other, more pressing affairs on the legislators' minds. And ship-wrecked immigrants were not yet taxpayers and voters. So it usually took a great disaster before there was any opening of the purse strings of Congress.

There were two such disasters in 1854. The *Powhattan,* out of Bremerhaven, Germany, with 340 persons on board, struck the outer sandbar off the New Jersey coast in a freak April snowstorm. All day long, rescue attempts were made, but the ship was too far out. Clinging to whatever they could, terrified passengers waited for rescue that never came. Slowly, one after the other, in twos and threes, they dropped into the sea to drown. Late in the afternoon, a giant wave swept over the ship and drowned all those still clinging to life. Not one person survived.

Congress acted by appropriating some money to build more stations and recommended that more responsible volun-teers be appointed, a would-be solution which barely met the problem.

Then another ship bearing over 500 German immigrants grounded 500 yards off Deal Beach in New Jersey. Her master and three crewmen fought the passengers for a lifeboat and rowed themselves ashore to safety, leaving the bewildered and frightened passengers behind. Lifesaving equipment was brought to the wreck, but by the time it arrived, night had fallen. Then it was discovered that the wreck was out of range of the eprouvette mortar. By morning, however, the ship had worked closer to shore, and an attempt was made to shoot out a line. But the mortar's springs had corroded and parted. The rescuers tried again and again until all the shot lines were used. They never did get a line out to the ship,

People began jumping off the ship, and many were washed away. But 163 people managed to make it to safety with the help of the lifesavers who went into the water after them.

As a result of this disaster, the Revenue Marine was told to investigate the shortcomings of the lifesaving system. They were easy enough to see. Equipment wasn't maintained properly because volunteers didn't see this as part of their work. Stations were still spaced too far apart, and the success of a rescue depended on whether a ship went down close to a station or five miles away from it. And Captain Ottinger's recommendations for the periodic inspections of the equipment by patrolling revenue cutters, and for money for routine upkeep and maintenance, had long gone unheeded by the Secretary of Treasury.

Congress heard all this, and it acted by authorizing keepers a salary of $200 a year. Somehow they thought that that was enough to make the system more efficient. Instead, it made for more political plums to hand out. Some keepers were political appointees who knew little about surfmen or even boats. But even for experienced keepers the problem was not solved because crews remained on a volunteer basis. As one lifesaver reminisced, "if a keeper discovered a wreck, he . . . would have to tramp miles before he could get a crew together, and perhaps by the time they reached the station, the vessel would be broken up and all hands lost."

The outbreak of the Civil War brought other serious matters to the forefront, so the lifesavers had to make do. One fringe benefit of the war was that the surfmen got rid of the hated iron lifeboats. The Army Quartermaster Corps commandeered all of them except one, which they couldn't find because it was serving as a pig trough.

By the end of the war, lifesaving stations extended from Maine to South Carolina and the Great Lakes. There were lifeboat stations with paid keepers and volunteer crews in some port cities. Volunteers were paid $10 for wrecks in which lives were saved and $3 for all others. Finally, human life was recognized as more valuable than cargo! On the coasts of Georgia, South Carolina, and Florida, houses of refuge were established, with paid keepers and their families, all of whom were expected to search the beaches after every storm and "to bring to shelter all persons cast ashore." Clearly, the government was getting a lot of unpaid help, a situation they would have liked to continue.

But in 1870, Congress squeezed out some money to pay crews during the "wreck season," but only at every other station on the Jersey coast. This certainly didn't help matters much. Paying crews at every other station did not draw many volunteers to the alternate stations. And paying crews during the "wreck season" only was a sure invitation to extend the season.

It didn't take a year before this was changed. The federal government finally accepted its full responsibility to rescue the shipwrecked. Substantial funds were provided for surfmen at all stations, and for as long as they were needed. It is to the surfmen's credit that they didn't extend the season to gain a full year's employment until the turn of the century!

More lifesaving stations were set up, with six-man crews at every station. Inspectors from the Revenue Cutter Service checked the stations periodically, and the men were now subject to discipline—something they had to accept when they received payment for their services.

For the first time, the men were given a set of written regulations with standards for maintenance of equipment and techniques of lifesaving. Naturally, no one expected to make lifesaving a cut-and-dried procedure. But drilling as a team insured more efficiency under stress and allowed teams from different stations to work together because everyone did their jobs in the same way.

In 1878 the Revenue Cutter Service lost the lifesavers, who became the United States Lifesaving Service. But both services still belonged to the Treasury Department, and the head of the Lifesaving Service and the head of the Revenue Cutter Service were one and the same man, Sumner Kimball.

When, in 1915, the two services were again merged into one, the Coast Guard's Sumner Kimball was retired, but it took an act of Congress to do so.

Despite its status as a federal agency, the Lifesaving Service never became *federalized,* in the way that other services did. The stations remained local affairs, regarded by their communities with the pride of ownership. Surfmen and keepers, who were usually accorded the honorary title of "captain," were mostly local men, often members of the same family.

Here is an account from the log of Keeper Jerome G. Kiah of Point Aux Barques Lifesaving Station, Michigan, written about a rescue attempt on April, 22, 1880:

> . . . we shoved with all hands in their places in the boat. After getting outside the reef we found the sea heavier with an occasional *very* heavy one. We dodged and weathered them all right until within about a ¼ mile from scow and nearly one mile distant from nearest point of land. Suddenly, I noticed a very big sea coming for us. There was only time to straighten her so that she might take it head on, but it proved to (sic) much for her. It came aboard and completely filled her. As the sea was leaving I gave the orders to bail, (we had two bailing dishes aboard) but the men saw that her gunnals (sic) were too far below water as soon as the sea had left us. In a few minutes after she broached to and rolled over with us. We righted her and tried to work one of the oars to get her stern to the sea, but it was impossible her gunnals (sic) being so far below water and in a few moments she rolled over again. We righted her again but with the same result. I am not positive whether we righted her

again or not, but if we did not I think the seas
rolled her over several times, but of this I am not
sure. All seemed to have hope at first that we
could hang on until we got to the reef. Where we
thought we might touch bottom and right her up,
and get the water out. At the time she filled we
were distant from the reef about ½ mile. (A)bout
¾ hours after filling Surfman Pattinger gave out.
From that time until the last man finished—I
think it was about ½ hour, they all seemed to go
in the same way, gradually going off in a stupor—
something like being chloroformed—with one
exception they were all holding on the boat by
the life-lines or finders when they gave up. Slowly
their faces would drop forward until they touched
the water and in a few moments after their holds
would relax and . . . the boat would slowly drift
away from them. The exception was Surfman
Morrison, he left go his hold or was washed
away. When I noticed him, he was five or six feet
from the boat seemingly unconscious, his face
was slowly dropping. I sung out to him calling
him by name, but he never showed any sign that
he heard me and in a moment or two I saw that it
was all over with him. Surfman Dugan was the
last one to give up. Up to this time my memory
serves me very good. This must have been about
7 AM. From this time until about 12 noon I can
remember only very little that transpired. I was
found on the beach by Mr. S. McFarland and Mr.
A. Shaw about 9:30 AM . . . Crew all cold in
death. With the exception of Keeper.

The heartbroken keeper could not face the loss of all his crew
and, unable to perform his duties, soon resigned.

55

One family dynasty, the Midgetts of the Outer Banks of North Carolina, has been in the business of saving lives since the 1790s. Hundreds of this family were part of the nameless beginnings when no records were kept of livesaving or lifesavers. Seven Midgetts have been awarded the Gold Lifesaving Medal, the nation's highest award for lifesaving, and three others have received the Silver Lifesaving Medal.

Rasmus Midgett received his Gold Medal for an extraordinary feat of lifesaving on an August night in 1889. Riding his horse on beach patrol just before sunrise, he saw debris washing ashore. His suspicions aroused, he raced miles up the beach until he found the source—a ship breaking up. It was the American barkentine *Priscilla*. Bound for Rio, she had been caught by hurricane winds which tore her sails away and forced her toward Cape Hatteras, "the graveyard of the Atlantic." She had grounded violently and was badly wrecked; waves crashed furiously over her hull. The captain had his wife and small son with him, and his older son was acting as mate. They and the rest of the crew went topside, the captain clutching his little son with an iron grip. Suddenly, a giant wave swept all his family away—the young boy from his arms, his wife, and his older son. The rest of the men hung on desperately. Minutes later, the hull broke in two, and captain and crew were clinging to the afterdeck section when Rasmus Midgett found them.

Midgett knew he could not get to his station in time to bring back help for the men. As a wave receded, he ran behind it, getting as close to the wreck as he dared for fear of it rolling over him. He shouted instructions to the men to jump overboard, one at a time, just as a wave ran back. Midgett retreated to the beach before an oncoming wave, watched the surf recede, and shouted for the first man to jump. As the man went over the side, Midgett raced for him and dragged him to shore before the next breaker could sweep them away. Seven times he did this, each time successfully

56

carrying off a man. But the captain and two others were too badly bruised and exhausted to jump. So Rasmus Midgett plunged once more into the water, this time going up to the wreck and pulling himself up a line hanging from the torn rigging. Hand over hand, he worked his way to the deck. Then, a minute of rest—but there was no time to lose, no knowing when the hulk would break up further under the pounding of the surf. He picked up one of the men, slung him over his shoulder, slid down the rope into the boiling surf, and flundered his way to shore. Then he went back and did it all over again for the second man. And again for the third.

When he accepted his Gold Lifesaving Medal, Rasmus Midgett said, "Anyone would have done what I did. It was my job."

This matter-of-fact attitude characterizes the men and the Service. Here is a typical log entry, written on February 15, 1885, at the Sandy Hook, New Jersey, station:

> This day at Lifesaving Station all day John Myrick came from No. 3 Lifesaving Station and had dinner with us Schooner Lida Hancock came a shore this morning Between No. 15 and 16 L.S. Stations at 4:35 A.M. She went to Peses crew saved Joseph Riddle shot a wild Goos this morning on the Beach it wade 9 pounds we had clam chowder for Dinner.

They were matter-of-fact about their exploits, but they were brave and full of pride. This pride in themselves became visible when, on the Great Lakes, crews took to wearing uniforms something like the Navy's. Soon, a uniform was adopted for use throughout the Lifesaving Service, to the chagrin of the men who had to give up several weeks' pay for them!

Now they were in uniform and had become a federal

57

agency with close ties to the Revenue Cutter Service. Suddenly, the Lifesavers found themselves in a very peculiar position indeed: the middle of the Spanish-American War.

Cuba, only 90 miles from the Florida coast, had been trying for years to break away from its mother country, Spain. Armed rebellion had finally broken out. American sympathy was with the rebels, and irresponsible journalists played on that sympathy with distorted stories for their papers. War was averted for a while, but several incidents, including the sinking of the battleship *Maine* (with the loss of 260 sailors), inflamed public opinion. And some members of Congress made demands for war. President McKinley finally gave into the pressures, and the United States jubilantly entered into an entirely unnecessary war. Having brought the war down on their own heads, the population on the Eastern seaboard feared that the country would be invaded by the Spanish fleet. Naval ships, which included the attached revenue cutters, patrolled the Atlantic coastline. The Lifesaving Stations were organized as a network for a warning system. If the danger of invasion never materialized, if in fact it never existed, that didn't matter. Having the Lifesavers there helped the country feel secure.

The war was a confused but short one, and soon the Lifesaving Service was back to normal. There were the lookout watches, the beach patrols up and down the stinging sands in the storms of winter and the rains and heat of summer. And there were the usual meeting of patrols from neighboring stations and passing a marker to show that they were where they were supposed to be and not in a neighborhood bar. The men kept their equipment and their houses in order. And they drilled. There were boat drills—the self-righting lifeboat being a particular favorite with local sightseers. There were fire drills and resuscitation drills. And, always, there were rescues.

But the rescues were different now. The day of the great

*An early version of the self-righting lifeboat.*

*A crew launches a lifeboat from a two-wheel trailer at the U.S. Coast Guard Lifeboat Station in Cape May, New Jersey, during the early 1930s.*

sailing ships, often at the mercy of winds and storms, was over. The clumsy steam packets had finally grown up and overtaken the tall ships. If they wrecked, it was further out from the coast. Soon, gas-powered rescue boats replaced man-powered surfboats, much to the disgust of some of the oldtimers, who bluntly said "the danged thing is no good." They had forgotten the agony of strained muscles and joints, of pulling their hearts out against a surf determined to carry their alien presence back to land.

Now, too, there were a different kind of people on the seas. The expanding economy of the country had produced a new class of people, with enough money and leisure time for boating and for taking vacations at the resort hotels that were springing up along the beaches. These were the people the Lifesavers were rescuing. There were more drunks, drowned

*This U.S. Lifesaving Station at Salisbury Beach, Massachusetts, was built in 1897.*

or just doused. The rescues were smaller, but there were more of them.

For the 70 years between 1871 to 1941, statistics show that cutters and lifesaving stations rescued 203,609 lives and nearly $2,000,000,000 in property from shipwrecks and floods.

But the story of the Lifesavers isn't told in statistics, not even in numbers of lives saved. Their story lies in the wonder of some long-ago person who said, "These men . . . took their lives in their hands, and, at the most imminent risk, crossed the most tumultuous sea . . . on that bleak coast, and all for what? That others might live to see homes and friends."

As the men would say—"There's a distress flag in the rigging, and we *must* go." They would add, too, that nothing says that they must come back.

# 6

# THE WAR TO END
# ALL WARS

On January 28, 1915, the United States Coast Guard was created from the Revenue Cutter Service and the Lifesaving Service.

At the time, war was raging in Europe, a conflict set off exactly seven months before on June 28, 1914, by the assassination of the Archduke Francis Ferdinand of the Austro-Hungarian Empire. The United States government struggled to maintain neutrality and did not build its defenses to avoid giving provocation to the Germans. But the formation of the Coast Guard at this particular time must have been done with at least one eye on that new phenomenon, the submarine. German submarines, called U-boats, were attacking the ships of unarmed neutrals, whether they carried war supplies or not. Often, innocent passengers were on board. International laws of neutrality forbade this. No one denied the right of a country to keep supplies from reaching its enemies, but a captured ship was to be taken to port. Or, if this was not possible, passengers and crew were to be taken off before the ship was scuttled. Perhaps that seems a little naive nowadays, but at that time, breaking this law was unthinkable savagery to the United States. Eventually it led the country into war.

SEA RAIDS AND RESCUES

On May 7, 1915, off the coast of Ireland, the British passenger ship *Lusitania* was torpedoed and sunk without warning by U-boats. Over 1,100 people lost their lives, including 128 Americans. There was outrage, but still no declaration of war by the United States. Several other foreign ships carrying Americans were sunk by submarines, but a determined President Woodrow Wilson held on to a shaky peace.

The United States kept up a lively trade with the Allies, and the Germans retaliated by continuing to sink merchant ships, armed or unarmed, neutral or enemy, passengers aboard or not. German saboteurs infiltrated the United States, and port security became one of the Coast Guard's responsibilities after the Black Tom explosion.

Black Tom Island, off the New Jersey coast, was a storage area for munitions waiting to be loaded on ships in New York harbor. On July 31, 1916, a giant series of explosions ravaged the area, shattering windows in Manhattan's office buildings and in New Jersey homes for miles around.

This and other acts of sabotage, and the continued attacks on unarmed American ships, finally drew America into the Great War.

The newly named Coast Guard found itself, as before, attached to the Navy, this time to join antisubmarine units and to convoy cargo ships and troop transports.

On one convoy, a British collier, a ship built for carrying coal, was torpedoed. In danger of sinking, she was abandoned by her crew, who were loaded onto the escort cutter. Her American escort sent twenty Coast Guardsmen aboard the collier to try to bring her into port despite her dangerously unseaworthy condition. But that night, gale-force winds tore the stricken ship apart and she sank, taking eleven Coast Guardsmen with her. Winston Churchill, then First Lord of the British Admiralty, wrote his condolences to the United

64

States: "Seldom in the annals of the sea has there been exhibited such cool courage, and such unfailing diligence in the face of almost insurmountable difficulties . . . America is to be congratulated."

The U-boats continued to be a formidable force. Even the geographic isolation of the American continent was threatened, as new long-ranging subs ravaged shipping within United States territorial waters.

When a British tanker, the *Mirol*, suddenly burst into flames on the horizon only seven miles off the coast of North Carolina, she was seen by the crew of a Coast Guard station. The keeper and his men went to the rescue of the *Mirlo*'s crew, who were unable to escape the 500-foot flames encircling their ship. The Coast Guardsmen launched their rescue boat in a heaving surf which tossed them back on the beach time and time again in a kind of monstrous game. The men finally won their way with the water—only to be faced by a wall of flaming gasoline. The keeper found an opening in the flames when the wind shifted and brought the power surfboat through, knowing that the opening might close behind them and block escape. Seared by the heat, vomiting from the fumes of the oil escaping from the tanker, blinded by smoke, and in danger of shelling from the U-boat and of being hit by the debris of the *Mirlo* as it broke up, the Coast Guardsmen went back and forth into this hell four times to save 46 men.

The men were rewarded many medals and citations for this extraordinary rescue, and John Allen Midgett, the keeper, added lustre to the Midgett legend.

The "War to End All Wars" ended a few months later. The Austro-Hungarian Empire was destroyed, and the Germans ordered to pay reparations. A lawsuit dragged through the courts to force the German to pay damages specifically for the Black Tom explosion and another New Jersey explosion, since they occurred before the country was at war. The courts finally ordered the German government to pay the United States $50,000,000. But by this time, it was 1940, and a different German government was involved in a different conflict: World War II.

# 7

# WORLD WAR II

When the United States entered the war this time, the Coast Guard was in good fighting shape thanks to the Prohibition era. Money had been poured into the Coast Guard for cutters and planes—a new air arm to stop the "rum-runners" who were smuggling in whiskey.

Even before Pearl Harbor, war preparations were being made. The Coast Guard organized the Greenland Patrol as part of a continental defense system. Greenland, the largest island in the world and a possession of Denmark, straddles the Arctic circle. But it is geographically close to Canada and of importance to the defense of the North American continent. Coast Guard cutters—including the incredibly tough old *Bear* —were joined by ten trawlers from the New England fishing fleet. They were manned by their owners, members of the new Coast Guard reserve.

The Greenland Patrol broke ice to keep convoy routes open. They found leads, or breaks, in the Arctic ice pack for the ships servicing Greenland, and they brought supplies into remote settlements. They watched for U-boats and warned convoys of their presence, and they rescued torpedo survivors. They reported weather and ice conditions when the Interna-

*A Coast Guard officer stands vigilant watch as his
troop transport slides through dense fog into an
East Coast harbor.*

tional Ice Patrol was discontinued to take on other duties.
And they did air and surface reconaissance to make sure the
Axis powers didn't set up radio and weather stations in the
area.

A sled patrol of Eskimos, Greenlanders, and Danes was organized as part of the Greenland Patrol, and they uncovered evidence of Nazi activity. A German trawler, the *Baskoe,* was captured several months before the United States officially entered the war. The *Baskoe* was carrying electronics specialists—a scientist and a nurse who were setting up a radio installation to report on convoy movements. Later, a party of Coast Guardsmen found and captured the radio hut itself, the first of several such incidents on the strategically-located island.

Greenland was also the scene of the first Coast Guard patrol bomber squadron. Based on the cutters—a far cry from Hamilton's tiny boats—they acted as ice observers, convoy escorts, and angels of mercy in some of the world's most dangerous weather conditions.

A month before Pearl Harbor, the Coast Guard was attached to the Navy, but this time the cutters retained their Coast Guard identification and crews intact. Other Coast Guardsmen were mingled with Navy personnel. As in previous wars, a major part of the Coast Guard's war duty was escorting convoys of merchant ships and troop transports.

In 1943, the cutters *Escanaba* and *Comanche* were escorting the United States troop transport *Dorchester,* when suddenly—torpedoes! The *Dorchester* was badly hit and sank so quickly that only two of its fourteen lifeboats could be launched. The loss of the *Dorchester* is particularly remembered in history for its four chaplains: Rabbi Alexander D. Goode, Father John P. Washington, Reverend George L. Fox, and Reverend Clark V. Poling, who gave their life jackets to men without them and met death together in prayer as the ship sank.

The cutter crews worked frantically for more than eight hours in the black night. Under constant threat of torpedo attack, they pulled survivors from the near-freezing waters before the numbing cold could kill them. The rescuers went over the sides themselves to tie lines around the men too weak

*A Nazi waits to be saved, after his submarine was sunk by a Coast Guard convoy cutter.*

to hang on. Or, donning rubber suits to give them some protection against the killing cold, they swam to life rafts and towed them to the cutters. By sunrise, 299 men were rescued, but hundreds more died, many frozen in their life jackets.

Many of the rescuers were themselves to meet death

*A Coast Guardsman rescues a crew member of a
U-boat, sunk by depth charges and gunfire.*

71

*Members of the U.S. Coast Guard's Mounted Beach Patrol.*

shortly. Another convoy, another torpedo, another—or perhaps the same—submarine, and the *Escanaba* went up in flames. She sank so fast that no radio message could be sent. Only two of her crew of 105 survived.

Coastline defense was also largely the responsibility of the

Coast Guard. And though they gave it everything they had, there simply weren't enough members to guard the many thousands of miles of American coastline. In the early months of the war, German submarines operated freely along the Atlantic seaboard and in the Gulf of Mexico. The U.S. Navy destroyer *Jacob Jones* was sunk in broad daylight off Virginia beach. Thirteen ships were sunk in the last half of January, 1942; in February, four ships were sunk in the Gulf in four days; and 40 ships went down during May.

On May 9, 1942, the *Icarus* was investigating a sonar contact off Cape Lookout, North Carolina, when a torpedo exploded off its port side. The crew raced to their battle stations as the *Icarus* searched the waters, tracking the sub as it dodged westward. Then, the sonar sang out a sighting, and a retaliatory load of depth charges could be dropped. The sub surfaced, its crew scrambling toward their deck guns. The *Icarus* raked them with shells and gunfire until the U-boat crew went over the side to be taken prisoner.

Coastal security rapidly tightened after this. Coast Guard aircraft and the "picket patrol," small boats often belonging to Coast Guard Auxiliary volunteers—kept U-boats from surfacing, forcing them to return for fuel and supplies without accomplishing their missions.

Another Coast Guard heritage from the days of the Lifesaving Service were beach patrols on horseback and on foot. The patrols, often accompanied by attack dogs, guarded against infiltration by spies and saboteurs landing from U-boats.

On one quiet June night in 1942, beach-pounder John Cullen set out from the Coast Guard station at Amagansett on Long Island. He hadn't gone very far when he spotted four men at the water's edge. Hailing them, as was routine on beach patrol, Cullen moved in to question the men. "We're fishermen, from Southhampton," they said. "We ran aground in the fog." Cullen offered them the facilities of the Coast

*Coast Guardsmen surprised and captured 12 Nazis at an enemy radio-weather outpost in Greenland.*

Guard station for the night, but this seemed to make the group edgy and somewhat sullen. Cullen was aware that he had a problem on his hands. When one of the men offered him money to "forget the whole thing," Cullen made a fast decision. If these men were spies, his refusal to take the bribe might stir them into assault, even murder. So he took their money and continued his patrol until he could get back to the station and raise the alert. The four men were Nazi saboteurs who had landed by U-boat. Cullen's information led to their capture by the FBI. The saboteurs were the leaders of an espionage network whose other members were apprehended in Florida. The four men John Cullen discovered were put to death in the electric chair.

In 1943, the first air-sea rescue unit was established. Combining air and surface craft, it was charged with the responsibility of responding to all offshore crashes. Air-sea rescue relieved battle units of searching and rescuing—a job they very often didn't have the time to perform. The boost to morale was immeasurable. Now, survivors knew there was a good chance of rescue, instead of being left to drift at sea until the enemy or slow death overtook them.

The Coast Guard's lifesaving tradition lived on, even in war.

President Franklin Roosevelt, once Assistant Secretary of the Navy, was also a yachtsman who appreciated the Coast Guard's ability with small boats and fast runs. He personally appointed 50 cutters to carry on rescue operations after the D-Day landings on the beaches of Normandy. The cutters rescued almost 1,500 survivors of sunken landing barges from the water, all the time under heavy fire from Nazi guns.

The Coast Guard also manned the landing craft in the invasions of North Africa, Salerno, Anzio, Tarawa, Makin, Kwajalein, Eniwetok, Luzon, Guam, Saipan, Iwo Jima, Okinawa.

The first major invasion of the Pacific islands began at

*A Coast Guard-manned LST delivers a load of
supplies to the American Forces of Occupation
on a captured island in the South Pacific.*

*Coast Guard war dogs, shown here on guard and scout detail, were trained to bring in prisoners unassisted.*

Guadalcanal, whose loss to the Japanese soon after Pearl Harbor was a sore blow to the United States. Now the Marines were coming back to Guadalcanal, and Coast Guardsmen were landing them on the beach. On one narrow point of beach, a group of Marines were pinned down by Japanese gunfire. Coast Guard Petty Officers 1st Class Douglas Munro and Raymond Evans, on landing craft duty, volunteered to evacuate the trapped men. With a flotilla of volunteer boats,

*A marine is transferred by Coast Guardsmen to a landing boat off the shore of Iwo Jima.*

they crossed the bay to where the Marines were stranded. Munro took his boat up to the shore, ordering the others to stay out of the line of fire until he could work out a plan of operation. Raked by machine gun fire, Munro's boat brought off 30 Marines and transferred them to the "ferry" standing

*Coast Guardsman Douglas A. Munro received*
*the Congressional Medal of Honor*
*posthumously.*

*Douglas Munro's mother, Edith Munro, was commissioned a Lieutenant, junior grade, in the Coast Guard's Women's Reserve in 1943. In this photograph, Mrs. Munro is wearing the uniform of a Cadet.*

by. He had seen that the beach was too narrow to accommo-
date more than three boats at a time, and the Japanese were
closing in fast. So Munro set up a ferry operation, then
positioned his craft so as to draw attention away from the
evacuation point. The Marines—almost 500 of them and
carrying their wounded—crowded on to the boats. Then the
"ferry" took them to where the rest of the boats waited. One
of them grounded on the coral reef. Munro's boat raced over
and passed a towline, finally pulling the stranded boat free.
But by then, the Japanese had reached the beach and were
firing directly on them. Munro and Evans swung to answer the
fire. By the time one full pan of ammunition was used, all of
the boats were out of range of the Japanese. The whole
operation had taken only a half-hour. But Douglas Munro had
been hit in that final burst of gunfire. He lay on the deck, his
last words to Evans a question: "Did we get them all off?"
Reassured that they had, he smiled, and died.

Douglas Munro was posthumously awarded the country's
highest decoration, the Congressional Medal of Honor. And
in one of the war's most unusual gestures of patriotism, his
mother, Mrs. Edith Munro, enlisted in the SPARS.

The SPARS, the women's branch of the Coast Guard,
took their name from the Coast Guard's Latin motto and its
translation: *Semper Paratus*—Always Ready. The women
served in clerical positions, releasing men for front-line duties.
Disbanded at the close of the war, they were reorganized for
the Korean Conflict. And they were disbanded for good when
the Coast Guard went co-ed.

# 8

# THE WARS THAT WERE NOT WARS

A war-weary country had barely the time to celebrate peace when, in June, 1950, it slipped into a war that killed and maimed many thousands but was denied even the name of war: the Korean Conflict.

In this undeclared war, the Coast Guard was not attached to the Navy, but it was authorized to again maintain a port security program, two Pacific weather stations, and Loran (Long-Range Aids To Navigation) transmitting stations to assist ships and aircraft. A team of Coast Guardsmen was sent to Seoul, the capital of South Korea, to train a Korean coast guard.

The U.S. Coast Guard also helped its former enemy, the Japanese, start their own coast guard, the Japanese Maritime Safety Agency.

In the early 1960s, the U.S. Coast Guard assumed another new role, the Cuban Patrol, shepherding refugees fleeing the Castro government. They came in all kinds of crafts, many of them unseaworthy, across the 90 miles of water between Cuba and Key West, Florida. Cutters refueled their boats and fed and nursed the hungry and ill. At the same time, the Patrol prevented American-based exiles from transporting men and arms back to Cuba, to avoid a provocation which might have led to war.

The United States was already becoming increasingly involved in another civil war being fought on the other side of the world in Viet Nam. Although it too was never declared a war, nevertheless it was, and many thousands suffered and died there.

The Coast Guard was ordered into Viet Nam to assist the Navy. Cutters participated in hundreds of missions in support of ground troops and to prevent supplies and troops from the north coming down the waterways to reinforce the Viet Cong in the south.

In May, 1966, the cutter *Point Grey* spotted what looked like two signal fires on a beach. She doused her lights and waited. Radar blips indicated a metal-hulled ship was coming in. The *Point Grey* challenged the ship, a 125-foot trawler, and forced it aground. But now the cutter was caught between the trawler and the Viet Cong on shore. They fought from dawn until mid-afternoon, when aircraft and other cutters came to the *Point Grey*'s assistance. Salvage crews recovered some 15 tons of weapons and ammunition from the trawler; about 80 more tons had been destroyed in the battle.

The fighting in Viet Nam dragged on for many more years, but by 1971, all the Coast Guard cutters there had been turned over to the South Vietnamese.

The Coast Guard mission on other, peaceful fronts did not stop because of the country's involvement in Korea and Viet Nam. Considering the Guard's roots, it could not be otherwise. The Revenue Cutter Service brought a legacy of law enforcement and assistance on the high seas. The Lighthouse Service (which joined the Coast Guard in 1939) brought its concern with aids to navigation. The Bureau of Navigation and Steamboat Inspection inspected and regulated maritime operations. The prime mission of the Lifesaving Service of the Coast Guard was the saving of lives.

Finally, there was one home for all the agencies concerned with safety on the waters. It was a home that was to encompass many missions over the years—the most diverse of the uniformed services, even though it is the smallest.

# 9

# STILL A TOUGH JOB

Today's Coast Guard has inherited all the duties of its many ancestors, and more, such as oceanographic studies and marine environmental protection. But essentially it is still a matter of men, and now women, who care for and protect the

*A 44-foot Coast Guard lifeboat rides the crest of*
*a spuming wave.*

country's well-being on the waterways, and in floods. A little extra is thrown in now and then on land, and sometimes in the air, when their helicopters serve as emergency rooms for babies too impatient to wait for proper hospital delivery!

Now under the Department of Transportation, the Coast Guard fleet has grown from Hamilton's ten revenue cutters to 24 different *classes* of ships. There are four different sizes of cutters, ocean and harbor tugs, riverboats, lightships, and icebreakers. There are seven different kinds of aircraft, including the great, whale-like C-130s, whose tails open wide to take on enormous amounts of equipment. Because they can fly long distances, then feather two of their four engines to slow them down, they are good for spotting icebergs, people, wrecks, and wrongdoers.

Coast Guard stations still dot the beaches, although not nearly so many are needed as in the days before aircraft. They still have lifeboats, but they don't depend on oar power. And in areas of high surf, a lifeboat is usually a self-bailing, self-righting, diesel-engined craft. If you take a quick bite of air when you see a 60-foot high wave coming down on you, hang on for dear life, and wait it out while tons of icy water crash over you and leave you hanging upside down in the surf. This self-righting boat will bring you out safely every time. It takes courage—the same kind of courage that characterized keeper Jerome Kiah and the fabled men of the old Lifesaving Service.

Today's crews are better served by their equipment than were the old lifesavers, but the sea remains the same bitter antagonist. It takes courage, too, to stand in the open door of a helicopter while hauling in a rescue cradle. Or to jump onto a rolling wreck of a tanker—the nauseating stink of escaping oil reeking in your nostrils—and having to live on it for days, always under the threat of breakup or explosion as you fight to stop its cargo from contaminating the waters. Or being awakened in the middle of the night by an alarm signalling a search mission, to be on the water or in the air in 20 minutes,

*One of the Coast Guard's first powered lifeboats,
the 26-foot surfboat* Lady of the Outer Banks, *is
famed for her 1918 rescue of crewmen from a
torpedoed British tanker off the coast of North
Carolina.*

heading for who-knows-what. It takes a different kind of
courage, described in Lt. Ken E. Fisher's account of a U.S.
Coast Guard rescue mission to the *Spartan Lady,* a tanker
breaking up in heavy seas 165 miles southeast of New York.

> Friday, April 4—
> What's that? A tanker sinking? Hey, we
> can't sail, we got two generators strewn all over

the engine room and three-quarters of the crew on liberty. Besides the CO had two wisdom teeth cut out yesterday and the XO is on leave. No way!

How long? Well, the EO says we could slap 'em back together in three hours.

Okay, start the recall. We'll never get them all back. They aren't serious about this Captain? Besides sir, nobody has any spare underwear or socks. Say again, sir? Aye, aye, sir, taking in all lines.

Saturday, April 5—

Far out man! At sea with half a crew, no visibility and three tickets to the circus I can't use. How long can I go on one set of underwear and socks before they make me sleep out on deck? Gear in good shape though, with just enough guys on board to get the job done right.

*Spartan Lady*'s stern section still has the screw turning. The Firebush is standing by the bow section. How did those helicopter guys get everyone off in this weather? Miraculous!

Sunday, April 6—

Who's got the funny papers? An attempt to bleed the oil lines in the steering system results in lubricating the entire bridge. Well, it works.

A commercial tug arrives to try to salvage the tanker's stern.

Monday, April 7—

0130—The stern section sinks. What's our next move Captain? Yessir, we got firepower enough to sink ten tankers. We wait for district approval.

Permission is granted to sink the bow section. The three-inch gun crew takes their stations. We fire 21 rounds of inert ammunition, which produce 17 neat holes in the bow. We switch to explosive projectiles and register 21 hits, but still the thing won't sink. How long can she stay afloat after all that pounding?

We break for chow.

I spill my peas when the OOD pipes, "If you want to see her you had better look fast." All hands lay topside to witness the *Spartan Lady* go down in 2,540 fathoms of water.

Tuesday, April 8—

Weather is atrocious, but when you're heading home who cares? Had a seaman get seasick and lose his false teeth overboard. The supreme sacrifice.

Wednesday, April 9—

Ambrose! Sixty minutes from home. CO congratulates crew and says he's proud of us. Does he know that we're proud of him too?

We tie up. My wife and son are on the pier. They approach me from downwind. My wife appears to swoon. Son is wearing muffler scarf, shows indifference to me but wonders if I brought him a surprise treat from the sea. Wife regains her composure and suggests that daddy has some aged whale blubber in his pockets. I explain my linen situation and go home sitting on the trunk of the car. Tomorrow is "business as usual."

# 10

# SHADES OF MIKE HEALY AND THE *BEAR*

The old *Bear* was a sturdy ancestor to today's cutters and icebreakers. Today's Coast Guard missions in the world of ice are more comfortable and less dangerous. But they still require a hardy breed to carry them out. And today's venturers into the Arctic and Antarctic have a great advantage over yesteryear's: the helicopter.

The icebreaker *Glacier*, keeping open the supply lanes to bases in the Antarctic and conducting oceanographic studies in polar waters, was called to the assistance of an Argentine icebreaker, the *General San Martin*, which had stuck fast in the ice.

Trying to get as close as possible to the *San Martin*, the *Glacier* found herself blocked by ice 25 to 30 feet thick. Ice this thick is many years old, very compacted and hard, and the smaller icebreakers like the *Glacier* cannot break it up. They can only push it away, if there's some place to push it. This was the position in which the *Glacier* found herself.

Helicopters scouted for leads because the *Glacier* was blind in the ice. After a day's slow inching, backing, and ramming, there was a sudden rocking vibration through the ship. Engines were stopped. When morning came, divers went

*A Coast Guard cutter maneuvers between two icebergs in the North Atlantic.*

down into waters so cold a man would freeze to death in seconds if his protective clothing was broached. The divers carried makeshift spears to fight off leopard seals and whales. They discovered that two propeller blades, each weighing about six tons, had been broken. It seemed as if both the *General San Martin* and the *Glacier* would be spending the winter frozen fast in the Antarctic ice. Helicopters soon evacuated all but essential personnel from the *Glacier*. Then, maneuvering inch by inch, the *Glacier* crew turned the ship around so it could go back the way it had come in. It took twelve hours to turn around. Hunting for leads in the darkness with inadequate searchlights, it took a day to move ¼ mile. Then a gale came up and buffeted the ship until it seemed as if nature itself wanted to keep the *Glacier*. Finally, about nine days later, the *Glacier* reached the open water of the Antarctic Sound. It had been a close call. The *General San Martin?* She broke herself free about two weeks later.

There are icebreakers on the Great Lakes and in the Arctic. There is no more Greenland Patrol, but the International Ice Patrol is still going strong, tracking the icebergs calved from Greenland's glaciers. However, tracking icebergs is no longer done by cutters, but by C-130s. Cutters are in the Arctic, doing oceanographic research. They pass on information about iceberg sightings and help out when nasty weather prevents the C-130s from flying the patrol.

In this electronic age, computers are used to help keep track of iceberg movements for better predictability of their paths. Even with all our electronic devices and other marvels, the only way to prevent another *Titanic* disaster is to keep out of the way of these mountains of ice which nothing can destroy but the forces of nature.

Icebergs near the Alaskan pipeline terminal of Valdez may extend the Ice Patrol's duty from the Greenland-New-foundland area to the other side of the continent. Meanwhile, the Alaskan Fisheries Patrol stands watch. Carrying on the conservation duties of the old Bering Sea Patrol, the Alaskan Patrol protects the rich fishing areas of the 100-fathom curve of the Bering Sea and the Aleutian Islands chain. There are usually three to six cutters on patrol, often with a helicopter

*This direct bomb hit was made by a Coast Guard
plane during aerial iceberg destruction tests
northeast of Newfoundland.*

on board to increase the range of surveillance, and a C-130 to
fly long-range reconaissance.

The United States now has a fishery conservation zone
(FCZ) extending 200 miles out from the coastline. It protects

the fish and mammals of the 100-fathom curve in the Pacific, the Georges Bank in the Atlantic, and other areas which were being fished or hunted out. Mike Healy, in his fight to save the seals of the Aleutians, would have appreciated the change from the three-mile limit of jurisdiction of his time. The three-mile limit had been set originally because it was as far as a cannon ball could reach, therefore as much as a country could protect. A nine-mile contiguous zone was added in 1966, but it was generally ignored and proved difficult to enforce.

The law which set up the FCZ gives the Unites States control over all the fish and sea animals in it, except the migratory tuna. It is aimed at protecting local fishing industries, as well as endangered species, against the factory ships of Japan, the Soviet Union, Poland, and East Germany. These factory ships are equipped to stay at sea for months at a time. Fleets of small boats, with electronic fish-finding gear and open-end sterns, scoop up tons of fish an hour, bringing their catches to the factory ships to be frozen and stored or turned into fertilizer or fish meals. These foreign ships "pulse fish." In other words, they clean out whole schools of fish, including the undersized young, so that reproduction is limited, and species are depleted or even threatened with extinction, as are certain whales.

Eight regional fisheries councils have been set up to determine fishing quotas for all species of fish in their areas. The quotas are based on the species' ability to replenish itself and the economic needs of the fishermen. If this quota is greater than United States fishermen can harvest, then foreign ships are allowed to fish for a set amount, providing their countries sign agreements with the United States State Department and pay a fee of up to $5,000.

It is the Coast Guard's job, along with the Marine Fisheries Service, to inspect foreign fishing vessels to be sure they have their permits. Both foreign and United States vessels are checked on quotas. And—an important provision

97

of the law—the Coast Guard can prosecute wrongdoers. Previously, only the ship's home country could do that. Therefore, it was rarely done, with the exception of the Soviet Union which was strict with its fishermen.

Boarding a ship at sea is always a dangerous procedure. Areas of good fishing are usually turbulent—good for fish, but not so good for boarding parties. The Georges Banks, for instance, where the icy Labrador Current and warm Gulf Stream meet, lies on a relatively shallow bed, sometimes only 20 feet down. This causes gigantic breakers where water flows from the depths to the shallows.

A ship about to be inspected is not warned. She must be approached and boarded speedily so that there will be no hiding or dumping of incriminating evidence. From the time a boarding party approaches a ship and the SQ-3 (international flag for boarding) is raised, only three or four minutes lapse until active search is started.

Boarding, particularly in the North Atlantic in winter, takes skilled seamanship and teamwork. The small boats must be launched and retrieved from the cutters. And keeping the small boat close to the large fishing ship is no mean feat. Members of the boarding party have to make a jump for a swinging rope ladder and climb for what sometimes seems like a mile—hoping that a sudden wave surge won't send them smashing against the side—to be greeted topside by a not-always cordial captain.

Tact is essential, and a facility for making oneself understood to Germans, Russians, Japanese, etc., without knowing their language. When there is suspicion of a violation a search of a large ship can take days. The boarding crew has to remain completely serious and business-like. Even their food is delivered from the cutter so that there is no interaction between crews.

That's true of American ships as well. American fishermen have been known to be pretty feisty about restrictions on their fishing. In Seattle, two fishermen, enraged by a fishing law which allows Eskimos to fish for a longer period of time because their equipment is so much more primitive, tried to attack a Coast Guard cutter with a small brass cannon. The cannon would probably have exploded if it had been fired!

# *11*

# RESCUE

The primary mission of the Coast Guard, the one that takes precedence over all others, is the saving of life, the Search and Rescue (SAR) mission. The mission is no different from that of the days when the lifesavers walked the beaches with their lanterns or were mounted in their lookout towers.

But today's Coast Guard watches with a radio console and other sophisticated electronic systems ships, and planes. Coast Guard aircraft log some 25,000 hours a years on SAR missions, and they range far and wide. But it was the beach-bound Lifesavers who started to work with planes, almost as the egg hatched. Three surfmen were with the Wright brothers at Kitty Hawk on the day in 1903 when the first powered plane took off from the ground. And it was those three who saved the plane from tumbling over in the wind just after that historic flight.

The typical SAR mission, if any can be said to be typical, was that of a California sailor on a 30-foot trimaran, the *Jan*. She capsized east of Bermuda in high seas on a trip from the Azores to Newport, Rhode Island. Her lone occupant activated his emergency locator transmitter (ELT)—a small, battery-operated device, with a range of up to 300 miles. ELT

101

*A crewman in a Coast Guard boat watches a
Coast Guard helicopter drop dry chemicals on a
burning Liberian freighter in the Mississippi River.
near Phoenix, Louisiana.*

*An evacuation by basket hoist from a cabin*
*cruiser is made by a Coast Guard HH-3F*
*helicopter.*

can broadcast for up to five days on civilian and military
aviation emergency frequencies which are constantly mon-
itored.

The sailor settled back, opened a can of beans, ate them,

*An amphibious Coast Guard helicopter alights on
the water in the Straits of Florida to pick up
Cuban refugees from two crudely hand-made craft.*

and calmly awaited rescue. About three hours later, a C-130 out of St. Johns, Newfoundland, came clucking overhead like a mother hen. With the help of AMVER (the computerized Automated Mutual Assistance Vessel Rescue System), the Norwegian bulk carrier *Herring Mille* was diverted from its course to pick up the intrepid sailor, who finished his sea voyage in Philadelphia rather than Newport.

AMVER tracks the merchant ships of 75 countries. These vessels voluntarily report their positions at different points in their voyages so they can give assistance when needed.

AMVER is based on Governors Island in New York harbor, and so is the National Search and Rescue School. The latter is a joint Coast Guard–Air Force undertaking which has trained thousands of rescue personnel from over 35 nations.

Many members of the Coast Guard Auxiliary have also been trained at the school. The Auxiliary had over 46,000 members who volunteer their time, their boats, and their communications equipment to assist regular Coast Guard units in search and rescue. Auxiliary SAR units are responsible for saving almost 1,000 lives each year. Their contributions to lifesaving are also indirect and unmeasurable: they conduct boating safety classes and safety patrols and inspections.

The capsized boat, the overdue fishermen, the downed plane, the drifting life raft, the wind-tossed sailboat—a year will bring some 75,000 calls for the Coast Guard. Some 5,000 people will be saved from death, and at least another 150,000 will be assisted in one way or another. Hundreds of millions of dollars worth of property will be saved as well as an incalculable amount of heartache.

The Coast Guard also seeks to cut down the threat to life by educating the public. It also develops and tests new equipment, makes inspections, and gives recommendations for new legislation—an agonizingly slow process.

And today's Coast Guard, whose main job has been to protect people from the seas, is now protecting the seas from

105

*This aerial view from a Coast Guard plane shows
the bow of a U.S. containership imbedded in the
engine room of a Colombian freighter after a
collision off the coast of North Carolina. An
estimated 24,000 gallons of diesel oil spilled from
the Colombian vessel.*

*An airman in a helicopter from a U.S. Coast
Guard Air Station in Puerto Rico lowers a basket
to one of the survivors of a single-engine plane
crash near a tiny island in the Caribbean.*

*Fishermen are hoisted from their capsized boat at the mouth of the Columbia River into a helicopter from the Coast Guard Station in Astoria, Oregon.*

people. Research and antipollution programs are new roots the Coast Guard is putting down to minimize the damage to the marine environment: ocean drilling and mining operations, tanker spills, deliberate dumping, and leaks and spills from thousands of different sources that are the main pollutants of the waterways. Inspection teams are constantly

*The U.S. Coast Guard cutter* Coos Bay
*maneuvers her bow close to the bow of a steeply
listing British motorship to begin rescue of twelve
remaining crew members.*

watching potential sources of pollution. And strike teams are
always on the ready to fly anywhere in the world to protect the
marine environment—the water, the beaches, the marshes,
the fish, the sea plants and animals, the seabirds—because
nature, too, has run up a distress flag in the rigging.

# INDEX

# INDEX

113

# MAJIC
# MAN

*A Nathan Heller Novel*

# Max Allan
# Collins

A DUTTON BOOK

DUTTON
Published by the Penguin Group
Penguin Putnam Inc., 375 Hudson Street, New York, New York 10014, U.S.A.
Penguin Books Ltd, 27 Wrights Lane, London W8 5TZ, England
Penguin Books Australia Ltd, Ringwood, Victoria, Australia
Penguin Books Canada Ltd, 10 Alcorn Avenue, Toronto, Ontario, Canada M4V 3B2
Penguin Books (N.Z.) Ltd, 182–190 Wairau Road, Auckland 10, New Zealand

Penguin Books Ltd, Registered Offices: Harmondsworth, Middlesex, England

First published by Dutton, a member of Penguin Putnam Inc.

First Printing, September, 1999
10 9 8 7 6 5 4 3 2 1

 REGISTERED TRADEMARK—MARCA REGISTRADA

LIBRARY OF CONGRESS CATALOGING-IN-PUBLICATION DATA

Collins, Max Allan.
    Majic man : a Nathan Heller novel / Max Allan Collins.
        p.   cm.
    ISBN 0-525-94515-6 (alk. paper)
    I. Title.
PS3553.04753M35   1999
813'.54—dc21                                              99-13679
                                                          CIP

Printed in the United States of America
Set in Janson Text and Trixie Plain

PUBLISHER'S NOTE
This is a work of fiction. Names, characters, places, and incidents either are the products of the author's imagination or are used fictitiously.

This book is printed on acid-free paper.

*To Paul Thomas—*
*musical magician*

Although the historical incidents in this novel are portrayed more or less accurately (as much as the passage of time, and contradictory source material, will allow), fact, speculation and fiction are freely mixed here; historical personages exist side by side with composite characters and wholly fictional ones—all of whom act and speak at the author's whim.

". . . [A] comprehensive further examination of the so-called 'Roswell Incident' found no evidence whatsoever of flying saucers, space aliens or sinister government cover-ups."

—Captain James McAndrew
1997 U.S. Air Force
*Roswell Report*

"No quiet murmur like the tremulous wail
Of the lone bird, the querulous nightingale—
But shrieks that fly
Piercing and wild, and loud, shall mourn the tale. . . ."

—Sophocles, translated by
William Mackworth Praed

"I am a victim of the Washington scene."

—James V. Forrestal
America's first Secretary of Defense